Reversing The Dummy

AND IT'S COUSIN, THE CROSSRUFF

JAMES MARSH STERNBERG MD (DR. J)

authorHOUSE

AuthorHouse™
1663 Liberty Drive
Bloomington, IN 47403
www.authorhouse.com
Phone: 833-262-8899

Published by AuthorHouse 02/28/2022

ISBN: 978-1-6655-5349-0 (sc)
ISBN: 978-1-6655-5348-3 (e)

Also by James Marsh Sternberg

Playing to Trick One; No Mulligans in Bridge (2nd Ed)
Trump Suit Headaches; Rx for Declarers & Defenders
The Finesse; Only a Last Resort
Blocking and Unblocking
Shortness – A Key to Better Bidding (2nd Ed)
When Michaels Met the Unusual
Zero to Three Hundred – A Bridge Journey
Reversing the Dummy

James Sternberg With Danny Kleinman

Second Hand High; Third Hand Not So High
An Entry, An Entry; My Kingdom for an Entry
L – O – L Loser on Loser
In Search of a Second Suit
Elimination and Endplay

CONTENTS

DEDICATION

This One's For:

DANNY
KLEINMAN

My Friend and Frequent Co-Author
Who Has Made My Books Better
By Being 'DANNY'

ACKNOWLEDGEMENTS

This book would not have been possible without the help of several friends. Frank Stewart, Michael Lawrence, Anne Lund, and Eddie Kantar, all provided suggestions for material for the book.

I am forever indebted to Hall of Famer Fred Hamilton and the late Allan Cokin and Bernie Chazen, without whose guidance and teaching I could not have achieved whatever success I have had in bridge.

I want to thank my editor Willie Fuchs, who makes my writing much better than it really is.

And Vickie Lee Bader, whose love and patience helped guide me thru the many hours of this endeavor.

James Marsh Sternberg, MD
Palm Beach Gardens, FL
mmay001@aol.com

INTRODUCTION

When discussing declarer play, the first thing I always suggest is for declarer to try to determine what kind of hand he is dealing with. Proper play of the hand starts with planning your play at Trick 1. After identifying/counting your losers, you need to look for ways to eliminate them. Counting winners too sometimes makes things easier, especially for dummy reversals. After all, there are only a finite number of types of hands, with variations on the themes. Typical hand types include a finesse, ruffing some losers in the dummy, setting up a second suit, a crossruff, and a few others.

But usually when I add a squeeze or dummy reversal to the list, that's when I find I have lost their attention. Dummy reversals are much easier to execute than most squeezes but often harder to recognize. Yes, perhaps the latter two are a bit more complex. This book is going to simplify the dummy reversal for you.

Assume you are playing in a suit contract. Spades are trump and you hold in hand:

♠ A K Q 3 2   opposite   ♠ 6 5 4.
♡ 5   opposite   ♡ 4 3 2

You will take five tricks, with a normal 3-2 trump split. On the other hand, with

♠ A K Q 3 2   opposite   ♠ 6 5 4
♡ 5 4 3   opposite   ♡ 2

You will take one or two extra tricks, depending on how many times you can ruff a heart before drawing the opponent's trumps. Trumping in declarer's hand in the first example, the one with the longer trump holding, does not increase the number of tricks. In fact, making declarer ruff too often may result in loss of control of the deal, a frequent defensive technique of tapping the declarer. In such cases, shortness is a detriment, not an asset.

When this technique is reversed, when declarer uses trump cards from his hand for ruffing and retains the trumps in dummy to draw the opponent's trumps, this is called a "Dummy Reversal."

The purpose of this is to produce more tricks than the normal play would have achieved. In effect, the dummy becomes the master hand. You can almost think of yourself getting up from the table and sitting on the other side. Now you are playing the hand from that side of the table.

Suppose you needed six tricks from the following trump suit to make your contract.

West: ♡ A K Q   East: ♡ 10 8 6 4 2

Suppose you are forced to ruff in the West hand. You could cash the remaining two high honors. If the jack falls, you have six tricks. By contrast, you could try ruffing three times in the long trump suit, turning it into the short side.

For example:

West ♡ A K Q   East ♡ 10 8 6 4 2
      ◊ A 6 4 2   ◊ 3

Play a diamond to the ace and ruff a diamond. Play a trump to the ace and ruff a diamond, then another trump to the king and ruff your last diamond. Return to the West hand in another suit and draw the last trump. Six trump tricks.

In effect, the long trump holding becomes the short trump holding after enough ruffs are taken. To accomplish this, one needs 1) to be able to ruff enough times to make the 'long' hand the 'short' hand, and 2) sufficient high trumps in the dummy to later draw the opponent's trumps. The coming examples will make this easier to appreciate.

What conditions facilitate a Dummy Reversal, to allow an increased number of tricks than the normal technique of ruffing in the dummy?

1. Shortness in declarer's hand, a singleton or void, with length in the dummy in that suit

2. Loser(s) in declarer's hand that cannot be ruffed in the dummy

3. Sufficient entries to the dummy; 1 per ruff and 1 more to draw trumps.

4. A large number of winning trumps that declarer can afford to ruff often in hand until the dummy has more trumps with which to draw the outstanding trumps, usually 3+ with 2 honors.

Here is a typical trump layout:

Dummy: ♠ K Q 2

Declarer: ♠ A 6 5 4 3

Usually, declarer will play low to the king and queen then back to the ace. With two trumps left over, he scores five tricks.

Ruffs in the short hand are always beneficial and provide extra tricks. If you could ruff anything with the ♠2 before drawing trumps, that would produce an extra trick. Ruffing with the ♠K or ♠Q would not since that would promote the ♠J for the opponents. You might obtain six tricks by ruffing with the ♠2.

But watch what happens if you get three ruffs in your own hand (declarer) instead. Now the remaining trumps look like this:

Dummy: ♠ K Q 2

Declarer: ♠ A 6

Now when you draw the opponent's trumps, discarding a loser from your hand on dummy's third trump, how many tricks have you taken? Six- the last three high ones plus three ruffs in hand.

An interesting sidelight is that often the best defense is 'tapping' the declarer, making him use up his trump. While this is often the case, if you are trying for a dummy reversal, the opponents are actually helping you with this defense.

By the time they realize it, it is often too late. Usually, the best defense against a dummy reversal is similar to that against a cross-ruff- repeated trump leads.

Let's look at a whole deal to see the benefits of a dummy reversal.

<pre>
                    ♠ J 10 9
                    ♡ J 5 2
                    ◊ Q 8 7
                    ♣ A 6 4 2
     ♠ 6 4 3   ♠ 8 2
     ♡ K Q 8 4   ♡ A 10 7
     ◊ 6 4   ◊ J 10 9 5
     ♣ K J 10 8   ♣ Q 9 7 5
                    ♠ A K Q 7 5
                    ♡ 9 6 3
                    ◊ A K 3 2
                    ♣ 3
</pre>

North-South reach 4♠. The defense cashes three rounds of hearts and switches to a club. If declarer draws trumps, he is relying on a 3-3 diamond split. However, if he can ruff three losing clubs, the fourth diamond can be discarded on dummy's third spade. This line will succeed when trumps are 3-2, a much more likely possibility.

Win the club ace and ruff a club high. A trump to dummy and ruff another club high. A trump to dummy and ruff the final club. Now cross to dummy's diamond queen. The position now is:

Dummy: ♠ 9 ♡ void ◊ 8 7 ♣ void

Declarer: ♠ void ♡ void ◊ A K 3 ♣ void

Declarer draws the last trump with dummy's ♠9, discarding his losing diamond.

How To Recognize A Deal Suitable For A Dummy Reversal?

1) Shortness in declarer's hand with length in same suit in dummy

2) Loser(s) in declarer's hand that cannot be ruffed or discarded

3) Adequate trump strength and length in dummy, usually at least two honors

4) Entries to dummy outside the trump suit

A Typical Example:

Dummy	Declarer
♠ A K J	♠ Q 10 8 5 3
♡ A 8 5 4	♡ 6
◊ A K 2	◊ 9 5 4
♣ A 6 4	♣ J 8 5 3

The contract is 4♠.   Opening lead: ♠ 4

Declarer has nine top tricks, including five trump tricks. But he has no chance of ruffing a club in dummy as defenders will deprive it of trumps each time they regain the lead.

The solution is ruffing hearts in declarer's hand, until declarer has fewer trumps than the dummy.

At Trick 2, cash the ♡A and ruff a heart. Enter dummy with the ♣A and ruff another heart. Cross again to dummy with the ◊A and ruff the last heart.

Declarer now has taken three trump ruffs in hand, and will take three trump tricks in the dummy. That's six trump tricks plus the four top tricks.

The only necessary assumption is trumps dividing 3-2, the most common division of five outstanding cards.

Classic Dummy Reversal

```
                    ♠ 9 8 7 6
                    ♡ A 10 2
                    ♢ K Q 2
                    ♣ A 4 3
♠ A J 10 4                            ♠ K Q 3 2
♡ 8 7                                 ♡ 6 4 3
♢ J 10 3                              ♢ 7 6 5 4
♣ J 7 6 5                             ♣ 10 8
                    ♠ 5
                    ♡ K Q J 9 5
                    ♢ A 9 8
                    ♣ K Q 9 2
```

North opened 1♣, South bid 1♡, and North rebid 1NT. South bid 2♢, New Minor Game Forcing in their methods and North bid 2♡. South's 3♠ bid showed shortness and slam interest. North appreciated his spade holding, checked for keycards and bid 6♡. West led the ♠ A.

West continued with another spade (not best, but) and South ruffed high.

This is a textbook example of a dummy reversal, rather than relying on 3-3 clubs.

Tr 3: Cash the ♡Q
Tr 4: Small heart to the ♡10. OK, Trumps are 3-2. Great!
Tr 5: Ruff a spade with the ♡J
Tr 6: Lead to the ♣A
Tr 7: Ruff the last spade with the ♡9
Tr 8: Lead to the ♢K
Tr 9: Draw the last trump with the ♡A, discarding the ♣9

Tr 10, 11, 12, & 13: Cash your winners, the four remaining high minors and claim.

Two Ways to See a Deal

♠ A 9 7 3
♡ Q 10 9
♢ 10 6 4
♣ Q 7 6

♠ K Q J 6   ♠ 10 8 4 2
♡ 5 3   ♡ 8 6 2
♢ Q 7 2   ♢ A K 9 5
♣ J 10 8 3   ♣ 9 4

♠ 5
♡ A K J 7 4
♢ J 8 3
♣ A K 5 2

North-South reach 4♡ after a 1-2-4 auction. West leads the ♠ K.

How are you looking at this deal?

Losers from the South side: ♠ 0 ♡ 0 ♦ 3 ♣ 1

Losers from the North side: ♠ 3 (avoidable) ♡ 0 ♦ 3 (unavoidable) ♣ 0

Tr 1: Win the ♠K with the ♠A
Tr 2: Trump a spade with the ♡A
Tr 3: Lead a small heart to the ♡10
Tr 4: Trump a spade with the ♡K
Tr 5: Lead s small heart to the ♡9
Tr 6: Trump the last spade with the ♡J
Tr 7: Lead a small club to the ♣Q
Tr 8: Lead the ♡Q, drawing the last trump, discarding a club from your hand
Tr 9, 10: Cash the ♣AK. If clubs are 3-3, discard a diamond. If not, you lose only three diamonds.

Consider Your Options

As declarer, when the dummy comes down, before playing to Trick 1, what should you be thinking about? What kind of deal is this, and formulate a plan accordingly. Often there may be several options, some better than others. The only real crime is to plow ahead with no plan at all.

Consider this deal:

```
                    ♠ A 7 6 2
                    ♡ Q J 9
                    ◊ Q 10 4
                    ♣ 5 4 2
     ♠ K Q J 5                        ♠ 10 8 4 3
     ♡ 4 3 2                          ♡ 6 5
     ◊ 8 5                            ◊ 9 7 6 3 2
     ♣ A Q J 9                        ♣ K 10
                    ♠ 9
                    ♡ A K 10 8 7
                    ◊ A K J
                    ♣ 8 7 6 3
```

South reaches 4♡ after a 1-2-4 auction. West leads the ♠ K.

You count your losers. What can you do to be sure to lose only three and not four club tricks?

One plan is to win Trick 1 and lead a club. You will lead a club at every opportunity, hoping to ruff the fourth club in dummy if either opponent still has a club. If clubs are 3-3, your last club is good.

This seems like a good plan but unless you are playing against sleeping opponents, they will lead trumps at every opportunity. You lead three clubs, they lead three trumps and so much for that plan. But the player who wins the third club may not have a trump and you are OK.

However, a second danger is they may play diamonds and arrange a diamond ruff. A better plan is to reverse the dummy by ruffing three spades in hand. Count your winners if you do- three ruffs in hand, three trumps in the dummy, three diamonds and the heart ace.

An easy ten tricks.

Win the opening lead and ruff a spade high. Lead a low trump to dummy and ruff another spade high with the king. Lead the ten of trump to dummy and ruff the last spade with your last trump.

Cross to dummy by leading the diamond jack to dummy's queen. Draw the last outstanding trump, discarding a club from your hand. Cash the last two high diamonds.

This is certainly a better plan than the first one, but just takes a little imagination and experience to see it. In this book, we will practice a lot of these, with some variations, so you will recognize them at the table.

GENERAL PRINCIPLES OF DUMMY REVERSALS

There is one basic rule to remember. You must ruff in the long trump hand until you have fewer trumps than in the short hand. What does this mean? Let's look at some more examples.

Deal # 1

You reach 6♠ and the opening lead is the ♡A then the ♡K.

♠ A 10 3
♡ 7 6 3 2
◊ A 6 5
♣ K Q 8

♠ K Q J 6 5
♡ 8
◊ K Q 7 4
♣ A J 4

If you ruff the second heart and draw trumps, you will take five spades, three diamonds, and three clubs. That's eleven tricks but you need twelve.

You must reduce the number of trumps in your hand to fewer than the number in dummy. You need to ruff three hearts, not just the second one. Cross to dummy with your minor suit entries in order to do this.

Your hand will then have only two trumps after ruffing three times, but that means you will score three ruffs, then three more trumps, three diamonds and three clubs. That's twelve tricks.

Deal # 2

The contract is 4♡ and the opening lead is the ♣A then the ♣K.

♠ J 8 2
♡ A Q 5
◇ Q 10 6
♣ 10 7 5 2

♠ Q 7 5
♡ K J 10 8 3
◇ A K J 3
♣ 8

If you ruff the second club and draw the trumps, you will take five hearts and four diamonds for nine tricks. One shy of your contract.

You need to ruff three clubs to shorten your trump suit to have fewer trumps than the dummy. Cross to dummy with a diamond at Trick 3 and ruff a second club. Next lead a trump to dummy so you can ruff another club. Now your trumps in-hand are fewer than dummy's so it's time to draw the opponent's trumps.

When you finish, you will have taken three ruffs, three hearts when you draw trumps, and four diamond tricks. That's ten tricks and your contract.

Deal # 3

♠ J
♡ Q J 7 4 2
◊ 7 3 2
♣ J 8 7 5

♠ A 7 6 5
♡ A K 10
◊ A K 4
♣ A 6 2

Yes, 3NT would be easy but you are in 4♡. The opening lead is the ♣ K.

If you win the opening lead and draw trumps, you will finish with the nine tricks you started with. So we need delay drawing trumps and find a tenth trick.

Guess what we are going to try for? Good guess. Win the opening lead and cash the ♠A. Ruff a spade and come back to your hand. Ruff another spade and----do it again. And again, the last spade.

Now the dummy has fewer trump than you do in your hand. Draw the trumps and cash the rest of your winners.

You will have taken the spade ace, three spade ruffs, three trump tricks when you draw trumps, two top diamonds and the club ace.

Add'em up. It's magic. Ten tricks.

Deal # 4

♠ 9 8 5 3
♡ K J 10
◊ A 7 6
♣ A 7 6

♠ void
♡ A Q 9 6 5
◊ K 5 2
♣ J 9 5 4 3

The contract is 4♡ and the opening lead is the ♠ A.

This is a matter of counting your tricks carefully. Ruff the opening lead with a high trump. Cross to dummy with a low trump and ruff another spade high. Cash the diamond king and cross back to dummy with a minor ace and ruff a third spade.

Back to dummy with your other minor ace and ruff the last spade with your last trump.

You have taken the first eight tricks. There are two high trumps left in the dummy.

Deal # 5

♠ K 5 2
♡ 10 9 4
◊ Q 5 2
♣ A 10 4 3

♠ 8 4
♡ A K Q J 7
◊ A K 4 3
♣ 5 2

The contract is 4♡ and the opening lead is the ♠ J.

The opponents take the first two spade tricks and you ruff the third spade high, the carefully preserved seven! Since 3-3 diamonds is against the odds, you try for a dummy reversal.

Lead a club and duck. Whatever the opponents return, you are in control (keep that heart seven). You can play the club ace and ruff a club (not with the seven), cross to the diamond queen and ruff the last club (not with the heart seven).

Now cash the high trump in your hand and lead the heart seven to dummy to draw the remaining trump.

Three ruffs in hand, a high trump in hand, two trumps in the dummy, three high diamonds and the club ace for ten tricks. Very well done.

Sorry, you got an average. Diamonds were 3-3 and all that work for nothing. Everyone else just drew trumps and played the top diamonds. No justice.

CHAPTER ONE

EXAMPLE DEALS

DEAL # 1   EASY TEN

```
                    ♠ K Q J
                    ♡ A 7 5 3
                    ◇ A 6 2
                    ♣ A 6 4
    ♠ 9 2                          ♠ 8 7 6
    ♡ K J 8                        ♡ Q 10 9 6 2
    ◇ Q J 10 9                     ◇ 5 4 3
    ♣ K 10 9 8                     ♣ Q 7
                    ♠ A 10 5 4 3
                    ♡ 4
                    ◇ K 8 7
                    ♣ J 5 3 2
```

North-South reached 4♠ after North opened 1♣ and South bid 1♠. West led the ♠ 2.

Without much of a plan, declarer, having been taught to "get the kiddies off the street" drew trumps and then gave the hand some thought. He lost one diamond and three club tricks, down one. North was left speechless.

What do you think North wanted to say?

Declarer can win the opening lead and cash the heart ace. Now ruff a heart high and cross to dummy with a low trump. Another heart is ruffed high and back to dummy with the diamond ace. Ruff the last heart. Declarer can cross to the club ace and draw the last trump.

She takes three trumps in dummy, three heart ruffs, three side aces and one king. Ten tricks.

DEAL # 2   TOO AMBITIOUS?

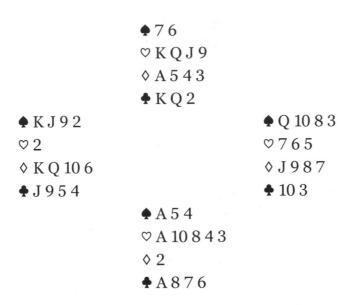

                ♠ 7 6
                ♡ K Q J 9
                ◊ A 5 4 3
                ♣ K Q 2

♠ K J 9 2   ♠ Q 10 8 3
♡ 2   ♡ 7 6 5
◊ K Q 10 6   ◊ J 9 8 7
♣ J 9 5 4   ♣ 10 3

                ♠ A 5 4
                ♡ A 10 8 4 3
                ◊ 2
                ♣ A 8 7 6

South opened 1♡ and North bid 2NT, a game forcing heart raise. South bid 3◊, showing a singleton or void. After a few cue bids and a Keycard check, North-South ended in 6♡. West led the ◊ K.

Declarer won the ace and played two rounds of trumps. If trumps were 2-2, she could ruff a spade loser, and a club if necessary. But when trumps were 3-1, and clubs 4-2, she finished down one.

Was there a better line of play to bring home this ambitious contract?

Win the opening lead and ruff a diamond. Cross to dummy and ruff two more diamonds. Then declarer can finish the trumps with dummy's trumps.

Declarer scores seven trump tricks (three ruffs in hand and dummy's four), one spade, one diamond, and three clubs. Twelve tricks.

DEAL # 3   THANKS FOR THE HELP

```
                    ♠ 9 8 7 4
                    ♡ A 10 5
                    ◊ K Q 8
                    ♣ A 4 3
♠ A J 10 6                              ♠ K Q 5 2
♡ 8 7                                  ♡ 6 4 3
◊ J 10 3                               ◊ 7 6 5 4
♣ J 7 6 5                              ♣ 10 8
                    ♠ 3
                    ♡ K Q J 9 2
                    ◊ A 9 2
                    ♣ K Q 9 2
```

South opened 1♡ and North bid 2♣, game forcing intending to next support hearts. South bid 3♠, a splinter raise for clubs. To avoid confusion, North simply bid 6♡. West led the ◊ J.

Declarer won and drew two rounds of trumps. He then tested the clubs. If 3-3, he could draw the last trump. If 4-2 and the opponent with four clubs had the last trump, he could ruff a club.

When the third club was ruffed, he was down one.

Not a terrible plan, but what was a better one?

Declarer can win the opening lead and play a spade. If the opponents play back a spade, that will only help declarer who is planning on ruffing three spades in hand.

Twelve tricks, losing only one spade.

DEAL # 4   WRONG SUIT

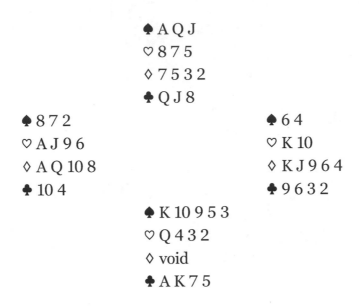

♠ A Q J
♡ 8 7 5
◊ 7 5 3 2
♣ Q J 8

♠ 8 7 2
♡ A J 9 6
◊ A Q 10 8
♣ 10 4

♠ 6 4
♡ K 10
◊ K J 9 6 4
♣ 9 6 3 2

♠ K 10 9 5 3
♡ Q 4 3 2
◊ void
♣ A K 7 5

South opened 1♠. North made a limit raise and South bid 4♠. West led the ◊A.

Declarer drew trumps and tried unsuccessfully to set up the heart suit. Down one.

Which suit should declarer be focused on?

The diamonds, not to set up but to ruff. With five spade tricks and four club tricks, the answer is to ruff as many diamonds as possible. Ruff the opening lead high, a trump to dummy and ruff another diamond. Cross again in trumps for another diamond ruff.

Now a club to the queen and ruff the last diamond. A club to the jack and draw the last trump.

DEAL # 5   NO FINESSE

```
                    ♠ K J 10 9 6
                    ♡ K 5 4
                    ◊ A
                    ♣ 7 4 3 2
     ♠ 8 7                              ♠ 4 3 2
     ♡ 10 8 6                           ♡ 9 7 3 2
     ◊ K Q 10 8                         ◊ 9 7 4 3
     ♣ A Q J 8                          ♣ 9 6
                    ♠ A Q 5
                    ♡ A Q J
                    ◊ J 6 5 2
                    ♣ K 10 5
```

South opened 1NT. After North transferred to spades, North-South reached 4♠. West led the ◊ K.

Declarer won the opening lead and drew trumps. He played a club to the king, hoping East had the ace. He took five spades three hearts, and one diamond. Down one.

Unlucky, the finesse failing, 50%, or was there a better line of play?

Much better. After winning Trick 1, lead a small spade to the queen and ruff a diamond. Play a heart to the jack and ruff another diamond. Now a heart to the queen and ruff the last diamond.

At this point, dummy remains with only the king of spades which you cash. Now play the king of hearts to your ace and draw the last trump.

You have taken the ace of diamonds, three diamond ruffs, three trump tricks, and three heart tricks. Of course you are hoping the club ace is on your left so that those who played the deal hoping for a favorable club position went down.

Score it up!

DEAL # 6   PESKY OPPONENTS

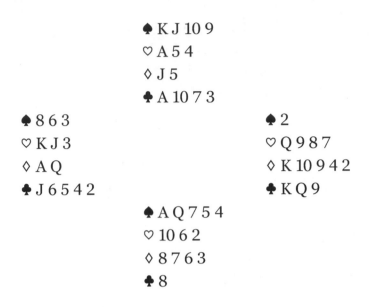

                        ♠ K J 10 9
                        ♡ A 5 4
                        ◊ J 5
                        ♣ A 10 7 3

♠ 8 6 3   ♠ 2
♡ K J 3   ♡ Q 9 8 7
◊ A Q   ◊ K 10 9 4 2
♣ J 6 5 4 2   ♣ K Q 9

                        ♠ A Q 7 5 4
                        ♡ 10 6 2
                        ◊ 8 7 6 3
                        ♣ 8

North opened 1♣ and South bid 1♠. North raised to 2♠. East pre-balanced with a take-out double and South, counting on North to have four spades, bid 3♠. West led a trump.

Declarer's plan was to ruff two diamonds in dummy. But unless the opponents were brain dead, how did he think this line of play could succeed? Back came another trump and when declarer led another diamond?

You guessed it- the third and final trump. Declarer could only ruff one diamond in dummy. Down one.

Ruffing yes, but what?

A better line of play is ruffing clubs in hand. At Trick 2, cash the club ace and ruff a club. Cross to dummy with a spade and ruff a club. Cross again with the heart ace and ruff the last club. for your seventh trick.

The two remaining high trump in dummy means you are making three spades.

DEAL # 7   LUCKY, LUCKY

<pre>
                    ♠ J 10 4
                    ♡ Q 6 4
                    ◊ A 9 7 6
                    ♣ A Q 5
    ♠ 9 6 2   ♠ 7 5
    ♡ A 10 8   ♡ K J 9 2
    ◊ Q 10 2   ◊ K J 8 5 3
    ♣ J 9 8 3   ♣ 10 2
                    ♠ A K Q 8 3
                    ♡ 7 5 3
                    ◊ 4
                    ♣ K 7 6 4
</pre>

South opened 1♠ and North bid 2♣, game forcing, planning to support spades on his next opportunity. South bid 3◊, a splinter raise of clubs. North bid 3♠ and South bid 4♠. West led the ♠ 2

This time declarer was lucky. After drawing two rounds of trumps, he tested the clubs. On the third round, East showed out but had no trump. Declarer continued with a fourth club ruffed in dummy. He lost three hearts, making four spades. Pretty lucky.

"Didn't you learn anything from the previous deal," asked North?

A better line of play is to ruff diamonds in hand. This requires three ruffs to gain one trick but there are adequate entries in dummy.

Win the opening lead in hand and play a diamond to the ace. Ruff a diamond and cross back to dummy with a trump. Ruff another diamond high and lead a club to the queen. Ruff the last diamond high and lead to the club ace. Draw the last trump.

This line of play is successful when clubs are 4-2, and will produce an overtrick if 3-3.

DEAL # 8   NICE SPOT CARDS

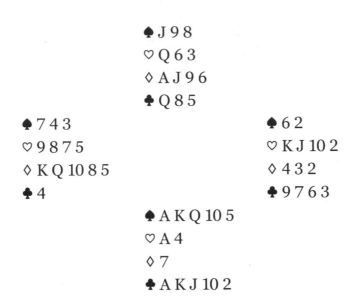

♠ J 9 8
♡ Q 6 3
◊ A J 9 6
♣ Q 8 5

♠ 7 4 3
♡ 9 8 7 5
◊ K Q 10 8 5
♣ 4

♠ 6 2
♡ K J 10 2
◊ 4 3 2
♣ 9 7 6 3

♠ A K Q 10 5
♡ A 4
◊ 7
♣ A K J 10 2

South opened 1♠ and North bid 2♠, a constructive raise. South bid Keycard and when North showed his one ace, South bid 7♠. West led the ◊ K.

Declarer had twelve top tricks. With no finesse positions, declarer ran his tricks, hoping one defender hah both the heart king and a high diamond and bared the heart king.

Sorry, Charlie. Down one.

Was there any play for this grand?

With the spot cards, declarer can make an extra trick with a dummy reversal. After winning Trick 1, ruff a diamond high at Trick 2. Then lead the spade ten to the jack and ruff another diamond high. Now lead the spade five to the nine and ruff the last diamond with South's last trump.

Cross to the club queen and draw the last outstanding trump with dummy's spade eight, discarding your heart loser. Cash the four high clubs for thirteen tricks.

Thanks for the nice spot cards, partner.

DEAL # 9   A MIRAGE QUEEN

```
                    ♠ J 10 9 5 3
                    ♡ 8 6 4
                    ◊ K 6 4
                    ♣ 8 5
      ♠ 8 6                              ♠ 7 4 2
      ♡ K J 9 5 2                        ♡ 10 7 3
      ◊ Q 10                             ◊ J 8 7 3
      ♣ K J 10 4                         ♣ Q 9 3
                    ♠ A K Q
                    ♡ A Q
                    ◊ A 9 5 2
                    ♣ A 7 6 2
```

South opened a strong artificial 2♣ and rebid 2NT after North's 2◊ waiting bid. North transferred to spades and bid 3NT, a choice of games. South bid 4♣, one try for slam in spades but North signed off in 4♠. West led a trump.

Declarer won in hand and played a diamond to the king. He finessed in hearts, losing to the king and West led another trump. Declarer won and played the ♣A and a small club. East won and led a third trump. Declarer ducked a diamond, West's queen winning. West led the ♣K. Declarer ruffed in dummy and cashed the ◊A. When the diamonds did not divide 3-3, declarer was down one.

"Sorry," moaned South, "The red suits were all wrong." "Finesse, finesse, finesse, when will it stop," asked North?

What was North referring to?

The heart queen is a mirage. At Trick 2, cash the ♡A and lead the ♡Q. West wins and leads another trump but now you can enter dummy with the ◊K and ruff a heart, the extra tenth trick.

Then the play is basically the same. You can enter dummy with a high club ruff to draw the last trump. Declarer wins five trumps, one heart, one heart ruff, and the three minor suit tops.

11

DEAL # 10   TWO WAYS TO SKIN A CAT

```
                     ♠ K Q 2
                     ♡ J 10 9
                     ◇ K Q 4
                     ♣ 10 7 6 2
    ♠ 6                                    ♠ J 10 9 8 7 3
    ♡ 5 2                                  ♡ 8 4 3
    ◇ J 10 9 7                             ◇ 8 5
    ♣ A K Q J 9 5                          ♣ 8 4
                     ♠ A 5 4
                     ♡ A K Q 7 6
                     ◇ A 6 3 2
                     ♣ 3
```

South opened 1♡ and West overcalled 2♣. After North bid 3♣ showing a good hand with hearts, South bid 4NT and found one keycard missing.

He bid 6♡. West led the ♣ A.

Declarer ruffed the second club and drew trumps. When he ran his trumps and high cards, poor West was squeezed in diamonds and clubs. Making six hearts.

Declarer was lucky to find West with four diamonds and all the club honors. What was a more likely successful line of play?

All the elements are present for a dummy reversal, needing only 3-2 trumps, much more likely. There are high trumps in the dummy and sufficient entries.

Ruff the second club with the ace of trump. Cross to dummy with a trump and ruff another club with the king of trump. Cross again in trump and ruff the last club with your last trump.
One last time over to dummy's ♠K to draw the last outstanding trump, discarding the diamond loser in the South hand.
Claim your slam.

DEAL # 11   WRONG SUIT

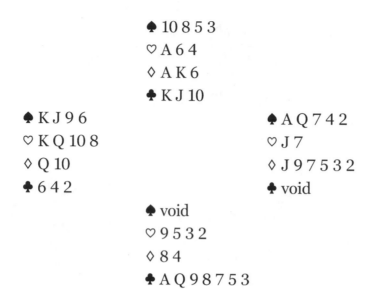

♠ 10 8 5 3
♡ A 6 4
◊ A K 6
♣ K J 10

♠ K J 9 6
♡ K Q 10 8
◊ Q 10
♣ 6 4 2

♠ A Q 7 4 2
♡ J 7
◊ J 9 7 5 3 2
♣ void

♠ void
♡ 9 5 3 2
◊ 8 4
♣ A Q 9 8 7 5 3

South opened 3♣ and North raised to 5♣. West led the ♣ 2.

South won the opening lead and tried to ruff hearts. He played the ♡A and a heart. West won and returned a trump. When West won the next heart, another club return meant no heart ruffs for declarer. He lost three heart tricks.

Down one.

A good opening lead but was the contract makeable?

Declarer was trying to ruff the wrong suit. Win the opening lead in dummy and ruff a spade. Now cross to dummy with a trump and ruff another spade. Over to dummy with the ◊A for another spade ruff, then the ◊K and a diamond ruff.

Finally, the ♡A is the entry to ruff the last spade. That's ten tricks and there is still a high trump in dummy.

DEAL # 12   THREE DOORS

```
                    ♠ 10 6 5
                    ♡ Q 10 9
                    ♦ Q 3 2
                    ♣ A 7 4 2        The Devil
    ♠ K Q 9 3                        ♠ A 8 7
    ♡ 5 4                            ♡ 8 7 6
    ♦ J 10 7 6                       ♦ 9 8
    ♣ 9 6 3                          ♣ K Q 10 8 5
                    ♠ J 4 2
                    ♡ A K J 3 2
                    ♦ A K 5 4
                    ♣ J
```

South opened 1♡ and bid 4♡ after North's single raise. West led the ♠ K.

The defense took the first three spade tricks and shifted to a club. Declarer drew trumps and hoping for a 3-3 diamond split, played the top diamonds.

About a 35-40% chance. Down one.

"Want to try again," asked The Devil? "But if you get it wrong again, you are mine." This time declarer drew only two rounds of trumps before playing three rounds of diamonds. He would succeed if diamonds were 3-3, or if the opponent short in diamonds did not have the last outstanding trump. A little better than 50%.

Down one. "You're mine," said the Devil, "Away we go."
Was there a Door Three? Would you like to try again?

After winning the ♣A, ruff a club high. Lead a small trump to dummy and ruff another club high. Lead the other small trump to dummy and ruff the last club with South's last trump.

Now cross to dummy with the ◊Q. Play dummy's last trump, drawing the outstanding trump, and discard your diamond loser at the same time. This door only requires a 3-2 trump split, about a 68% chance.

Did the Devil get you?

DEAL # 13   NO FINESSE PLEASE

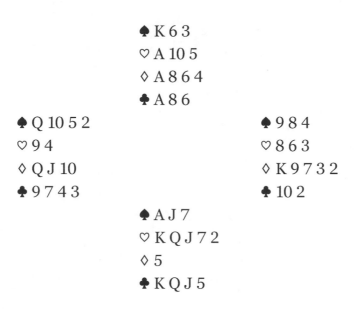

♠ K 6 3
♥ A 10 5
♦ A 8 6 4
♣ A 8 6

♠ Q 10 5 2   ♠ 9 8 4
♥ 9 4   ♥ 8 6 3
♦ Q J 10   ♦ K 9 7 3 2
♣ 9 7 4 3   ♣ 10 2

♠ A J 7
♥ K Q J 7 2
♦ 5
♣ K Q J 5

South opened 1♥. North bid 2♣ creating a game force, planning to support hearts at his next turn. South's 3♦ bid was a splinter raise of clubs. North bid 3♥. South cue bid 3♠ and North bid 4NT checking for Keycards.

After South's 5♠ response, North bid 5NT. South bid 6♣, the club king and North bid 7♥. West led the ♦ Q.

Declarer drew trumps and took a spade finesse. Sure, swift, and wrong.
Down one. "Partner, we are in a grand slam," said North. "A little more effort?"

What was North referring to? Was there an alternative line of play?

Maybe. Win the opening lead (good play) and ruff a diamond. Cash the ♥AK to see how the trumps divide. When they are 3-2, ruff another diamond leaving one trump out. A club to the ace and another diamond ruff with South's last trump.

Then cross to dummy's ♠K and play the ♥J, drawing the last trump and discarding South's spade loser.

Six trump tricks instead of five, four clubs, two spades and one diamond. By testing trumps early, declarer could take this line. If trumps were 4-1, he had the spade finesse as a last resort.

DEAL # 14   A LITTLE MORE EFFORT

```
                    ♠ J 9 8 7
                    ♡ 10 8 2
                    ◊ A 9 3 2
                    ♣ 9 2
♠ 6 5 4                              ♠ 3
♡ K J 4 3                            ♡ Q 9 6
◊ K Q J 7                            ◊ 10 8 6 5
♣ 8 5                               ♣ J 10 7 6 4
                    ♠ A K Q 10 2
                    ♡ A 7 5
                    ◊ 4
                    ♣ A K Q 3
```

South opened 2♣, strong and artificial and bid 2♠ after North's 2◊ waiting bid. North raised to 3♠, showing trump support plus something on the side. South cue bid 4♣. When North cue bid 4◊, South bid 6♠. West led the ◊ K.

South was stuck. He could draw the trumps and cash three clubs, discarding a spade. He could give up a spade and ruff a spade but would have a club loser.

Hoping for 3-3 clubs, he played three rounds but when the third club was ruffed, it was curtains.

Any other ideas?

After winning the opening lead, ruff a diamond in the closed hand. Cash two high clubs and cross to dummy with a low trump. Ruff another diamond high.

Now lead the spade ten and overtake with the jack. Ruff the last diamond. Cross to dummy with a club ruff and draw the last trump.

Declarer wins three high clubs, one high diamond, one high heart, three diamond ruffs, and four trump tricks in dummy. Twelve big ones.

DEAL # 15   WHERE IS THE TENTH?

```
                          ♠ 8 7 5
                          ♡ A Q J
                          ◇ 7 5 3 2
                          ♣ Q J 8
        ♠ A J 10 9                        ♠ K 6
        ♡ 6 4                             ♡ 8 7 2
        ◇ A K 9 6                         ◇ Q J 10 8 4
        ♣ 10 9 2                          ♣ 7 5 3
                          ♠ Q 4 3 2
                          ♡ K 10 9 5 3
                          ◇ void
                          ♣ A K 6 4
```

South opened 1♡ and after a competitive auction end in 4♡. West led the ◇ A.

Declarer counted nine tricks. Where is the tenth? Maybe spades are 3-3? Maybe, less likely, a spade ruff in dummy? The snag is that 3-3 is against the odds, and the opponents, unless one of your relatives, will start leading trumps every time they get in.

What is a better line of play?

You ruff the opening lead but that's not a tenth trick. That's one of your five trump tricks. But suppose you ruff three diamonds. Now you would get six trump tricks; three in your hand and three in the dummy. Can you arrange that?

Ruff the opening lead, cross to the ♡Q, ruff another diamond, cross to the ♡J, and ruff a third diamond. Now cross to the ♣Q and draw the remaining trump. This line only requires 3-2 trumps.

DEAL # 16　TRUMP CONTROL

```
                    ♠ 7 6 5
                    ♡ Q 10
                    ◇ A K Q 5
                    ♣ 10 9 7 6
♠ 10 9                                ♠ K Q J
♡ 9 8 6 5 3                           ♡ K J 7
◇ 9 4                                 ◇ 10 7 6
♣ K 8 5 2                             ♣ Q J 4 3
                    ♠ A 8 4 3 2
                    ♡ A 4 2
                    ◇ J 8 3 2
                    ♣ A
```

South opened 1♠. North showed a three-card limit raise by first bidding 1NT forcing, then 3♠ after South bid 2♣. South bid 4♠. West led the ♠ 9.

Declarer won Trick 1 and led a low heart. East won and cashed two trump tricks. South had another heart loser at the end. Down one.

Too high? Poor trump? Or misplayed?

By making better use of the trumps, declarer can take ten tricks with a form of dummy reversal. First, duck Trick 1 to keep control of the trump suit. Win Trick 2, probably another trump. If not cash the ♠A and cash the ♣A.

Using the diamonds as entries, declarer can ruff three clubs in hand. Whether the defense ruffs in or not, declarer loses only two trump tricks and one heart.

Ten tricks.

DEAL # 17   TRUMP CONTROL II

$$\spadesuit\ 8\ 7\ 5$$
$$\heartsuit\ A\ 7\ 6\ 2$$
$$\diamondsuit\ Q\ 7$$
$$\clubsuit\ K\ J\ 10\ 6$$

$$\spadesuit\ J\ 10 \qquad\qquad \spadesuit\ K\ Q\ 6$$
$$\heartsuit\ K\ 10\ 8 \qquad\qquad \heartsuit\ Q\ J\ 9\ 4\ 3$$
$$\diamondsuit\ J\ 9\ 4\ 3\ 2 \qquad\qquad \diamondsuit\ K\ 10\ 6$$
$$\clubsuit\ 8\ 7\ 2 \qquad\qquad \clubsuit\ 9\ 5$$

$$\spadesuit\ A\ 9\ 4\ 3\ 2$$
$$\heartsuit\ 5$$
$$\diamondsuit\ A\ 8\ 5$$
$$\clubsuit\ A\ Q\ 4\ 3$$

South opened 1♠ and bid 4♠ after North showed a three-trump limit raise. West led the ♠ J.

Declarer won the ace and led a low diamond. East won and cashed two rounds of trumps. South still had a losing diamond. Down one.

"Partner, we just went over a similar deal," lamented North.

What was North referring to?

First, declarer should duck Trick 1 to maintain control. Win Trick 2 and lead a heart to the ace. Ruff a heart and using the clubs as entries ruff two more hearts.

Declarer will only lose two trumps and one diamond.

DEAL # 18   WHAT CAN GO WRONG?

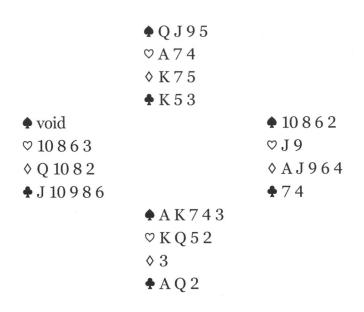

♠ Q J 9 5
♡ A 7 4
◇ K 7 5
♣ K 5 3

♠ void
♡ 10 8 6 3
◇ Q 10 8 2
♣ J 10 9 8 6

♠ 10 8 6 2
♡ J 9
◇ A J 9 6 4
♣ 7 4

♠ A K 7 4 3
♡ K Q 5 2
◇ 3
♣ A Q 2

South opened 1♠ and North bid 2NT, a forcing spade raise. South could have bid 3◇ showing shortness, but chose 4NT. North bid 5♣, one keycard. South's 5◇ asked for the trump queen. North bid 6♣, showing the trump queen and the club king. South bid 6♠. West led the ♣ J.

Declarer won the opening lead in hand and played a low spade, intending to draw trumps and ruff his fourth heart if necessary. When West showed out, there was no recovery. He lost a diamond and a heart.

What did declarer forget to do?

The old question, what could go wrong? Only a 4-0 trump split. To counter this possibility, you need to plan to ruff two diamonds in hand, shortening your trump.

Win the opening lead in hand and cash the ♠A. When West shows out, lead a diamond to the king. East wins the ace and returns a club. Win in dummy and ruff a diamond. Cross to the ♡A and ruff the last diamond.

Cash the ♠K and lead a low spade. Draw the last two trump with dummy's ♠QJ. Making six spades.

DEAL # 19   OH NO, NOT AGAIN

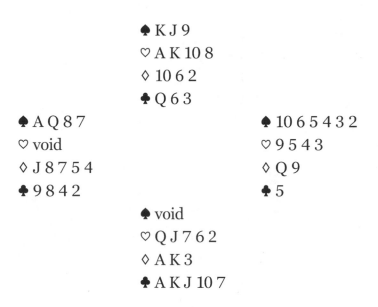

```
                    ♠ K J 9
                    ♡ A K 10 8
                    ◊ 10 6 2
                    ♣ Q 6 3
♠ A Q 8 7                              ♠ 10 6 5 4 3 2
♡ void                                ♡ 9 5 4 3
◊ J 8 7 5 4                           ◊ Q 9
♣ 9 8 4 2                             ♣ 5
                    ♠ void
                    ♡ Q J 7 6 2
                    ◊ A K 3
                    ♣ A K J 10 7
```

South opened 1♡ and North bid 2NT, a forcing heart raise. South bid 5♡, an old-fashioned grand slam force that if North had two of the top three trump honors, bid 6♥with one honor, seven with two honors, and pass with neither, North bid 7♡. West led the ♣ 9.

Declarer saw twelve tricks. What to do with the diamond loser? A squeeze lacked communication. Four rounds of clubs to discard a diamond? Unlikely.

Declarer won the ♣A and led a trump. West showed out. Winning the ace in dummy, declarer played for a dummy reversal, ruffing a spade. With a second spade ruff, he would succeed. But how was he going to get back to the dummy?

If he led a club, East would ruff. If he led a trump, East would score a trump trick.

What is one of the prerequisites for a dummy reversal?

Entries. If you win Trick 1 with the ♣Q and ruff a spade at Trick 2, you only need one more entry to ruff one more spade. Now you have two spade ruffs, four trump tricks, and seven top cards in the minors.

I think that's thirteen, no?

DEAL # 20   WHAT CAN GO WRONG?

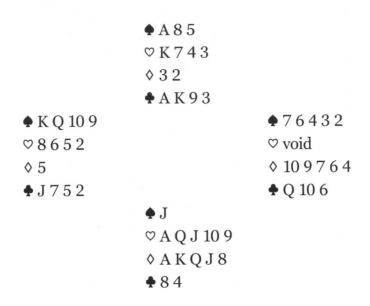

<pre>
                    ♠ A 8 5
                    ♡ K 7 4 3
                    ◊ 3 2
                    ♣ A K 9 3
    ♠ K Q 10 9   ♠ 7 6 4 3 2
    ♡ 8 6 5 2   ♡ void
    ◊ 5   ◊ 10 9 7 6 4
    ♣ J 7 5 2   ♣ Q 10 6
                    ♠ J
                    ♡ A Q J 10 9
                    ◊ A K Q J 8
                    ♣ 8 4
</pre>

South opened 1♡ and North bid 2NT, conventionally a game forcing heart raise. South bid 4◊, showing a very good second suit, a source of tricks. North bid 4NT, asking for keycards, then 5NT asking for specific kings. With that information, North bid 7♡. West led the ♠ K.

Declarer confidently and rapidly drew trumps and started the diamonds, getting ready to claim. When West showed out on the second diamond, play slowed to a halt. Down one.

Unlucky yes but avoidable?

Declarer forgot to ask himself what could go wrong? Only a 5-1 diamond split. As a precaution and as general good technique, ruff a spade at Trick 2.

Next draw three rounds of trumps and lead a club to the ace. Ruff dummy's last spade with South's last trump. Now cross to dummy's king of clubs.

Draw the last trump with dummy's heart king, discarding the diamond eight. The 5-1 diamond split is of no concern. Making seven hearts.

DEAL # 21   NO FINESSE, MORE RUFFING

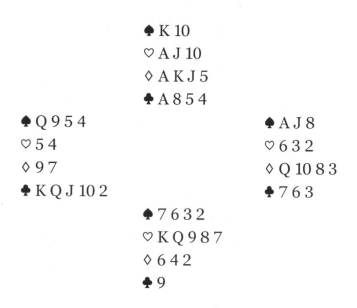

　　　　　　♠ K 10
　　　　　　♡ A J 10
　　　　　　◊ A K J 5
　　　　　　♣ A 8 5 4

♠ Q 9 5 4　　　　　　　　　　♠ A J 8
♡ 5 4　　　　　　　　　　　　♡ 6 3 2
◊ 9 7　　　　　　　　　　　　◊ Q 10 8 3
♣ K Q J 10 2　　　　　　　　♣ 7 6 3

　　　　　　♠ 7 6 3 2
　　　　　　♡ K Q 9 8 7
　　　　　　◊ 6 4 2
　　　　　　♣ 9

North opened 2NT. South bid Stayman, then 3♡ over North's 3◊ response. North bid 4♡. West led the ♣ K.

Declarer won the opening lead and ruffed a club. Then he tried a spade to dummy's king. East won and led a trump. Declarer won and led another spade. East led a second trump. Declarer ruffed a spade but still had a spade loser.

He ruffed a club, drew the last trump and took a diamond finesse. When that lost and East returned a diamond, declarer had a slow diamond loser at the end.
Down one, losing two spades and two diamonds.

Could you have found a better road home?

After ruffing a club at Trick 2, forget about the spades, forget about finesses. Use the ♦AK as entries to ruff two more clubs. Then concede a diamond. Win the trump return in dummy and ruff the last diamond.

Add 'em up: Four ruffs in hand, three trumps in dummy, two high diamonds and one high club. Looks like ten to me.

DEAL # 22   PIECE OF CAKE

```
                    ♠ J 9 8
                    ♡ A 8 5 3
                    ◊ 6 5 4
                    ♣ J 3 2
        ♠ 7 6                       ♠ 4 3 2
        ♡ Q J 10 9                  ♡ K 7 6 2
        ◊ Q 10 9 8                  ◊ J 3 2
        ♣ 10 8 7                    ♣ 9 5 4
                    ♠ A K Q 10 5
                    ♡ 4
                    ◊ A K 7
                    ♣ A K Q 6
```

South opened 2♣, strong and artificial. Usually, three suited hands are best bid by starting with one of a suit, but with 25 HCP, 2♣ is reasonable. South rebid 2♠ after North's 2◊ waiting bid.

When North raised to 3♠, stronger than four, South checked for keycards and bid 7♠. West led the ♡ Q.

Declarer counted twelve tricks. He ran all his winners, but the defenders discarded properly. Down one.

Where there are twelve, there might be thirteen. Do you see it?

The ♠98 are big cards. They provide an extra entry for a dummy reversal. Win the opening lead and ruff a heart high. Lead the ♠5 to dummy's ♠8 and ruff another heart high. Cross again with the ♠ 10 to the ♠J and ruff the last heart.

The ♣J is an entry to dummy to draw the last trump, discarding a diamond on the ♠9.

DEAL # 23   PREPARATION

$\spadesuit$ Q J 5
$\heartsuit$ Q 8 4
$\diamond$ 6 3 2
$\clubsuit$ A K 9 5

$\spadesuit$ 8 6 $\spadesuit$ 7 4 2
$\heartsuit$ J 10 7 6 $\heartsuit$ 5 2
$\diamond$ K Q 10 9 $\diamond$ J 8 5 4
$\clubsuit$ 10 8 6 $\clubsuit$ Q J 4 3

$\spadesuit$ A K 10 9 3
$\heartsuit$ A K 9 3
$\diamond$ A 7
$\clubsuit$ 7 2

South opened 1$\spadesuit$ and North bid 2$\clubsuit$, game forcing. South bid 2$\heartsuit$ and North bid 2$\spadesuit$.. South cue bid 3$\diamond$. When North bid 4$\clubsuit$, South bid 6$\spadesuit$. West led the $\diamond$ K.

Declarer only had one loser in diamonds, but he only had eleven tricks unless hearts were 3-3. He drew two rounds of trumps and tested the hearts, East ruffed and returned a diamond. Down one. South started to make excuses but North said, "I don't want to hear it."

Was there a successful line South had overlooked?

Yes, but a little preparation is required first. After winning the opening lead, declarer should play back a diamond at Trick 2. Or declarer could duck the opening lead. What can the defense do?

If West shifts to a trump, South can win in hand and lead a club to dummy. Ruff the last diamond high and lead another club.

Now ruff a club high and lead a trump to dummy. Ruff the last club high, cross to the $\heartsuit$Q and draw the last trump. The $\heartsuit$AK take the last two tricks.

DEAL # 24   USING YOUR TRUMP WISELY

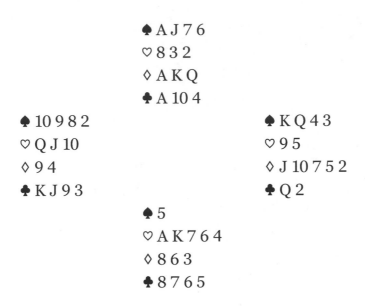

♠ A J 7 6
♡ 8 3 2
♢ A K Q
♣ A 10 4

♠ 10 9 8 2
♡ Q J 10
♢ 9 4
♣ K J 9 3

♠ K Q 4 3
♡ 9 5
♢ J 10 7 5 2
♣ Q 2

♠ 5
♡ A K 7 6 4
♢ 8 6 3
♣ 8 7 6 5

North open 1♣ and rebid 2NT after South bid 1♡. South bid 3♢, New Minor, and raised North's 3♡ bid to 4♡. West led the ♠ 10.

Declarer was looking at a trump loser, two probable club losers, and a fourth club that he might have to deal with. He tried to ruff a club and went down.

"If I draw two rounds of trumps first, West will cash the third round," said South. "How many times do you have to see these deals to get it right," asked North?

What was North referring to?

South could make better use of his trump by playing 'up-side down'. Win the opening lead and ruff a spade at Trick 2. Cash the ♡AK and reach dummy twice in diamonds to ruff two more spades.

Then play a third diamond. He will win two more tricks no matter how West continues.

DEAL # 25   GOOD TRY

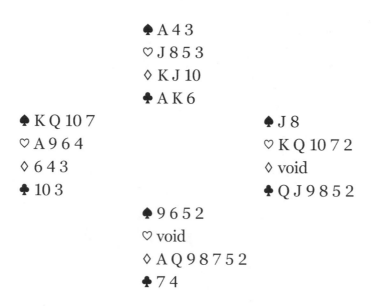

```
                    ♠ A 4 3
                    ♡ J 8 5 3
                    ◇ K J 10
                    ♣ A K 6
♠ K Q 10 7                              ♠ J 8
♡ A 9 6 4                              ♡ K Q 10 7 2
◇ 6 4 3                               ◇ void
♣ 10 3                               ♣ Q J 9 8 5 2
                    ♠ 9 6 5 2
                    ♡ void
                    ◇ A Q 9 8 7 5 2
                    ♣ 7 4
```

South opened 3◇ and North raised to 5◇. West led the ◇ 3. Declarer won and cashed the spade ace and conceded a spade. West won and played another trump. Declarer ducked one more spade but West won and led his last trump.

Declarer had a losing spade at the end.

Good opening lead, the ♠K would have made life easy. Can declarer survive?

The opening lead was inspired but declarer should take a different road. Trying now for a spade ruff was futile. Win the opening lead in dummy and ruff a heart.

Lead a club to dummy and ruff another heart high. Then another club to dummy and another high heart ruff. A spade to the ace and ruff the last heart.

Having won the first eight tricks, lead a trump to dummy (9) and ruff the last club (10). Dummy still has a high trump (11).

DEAL # 26   TROUBLE?

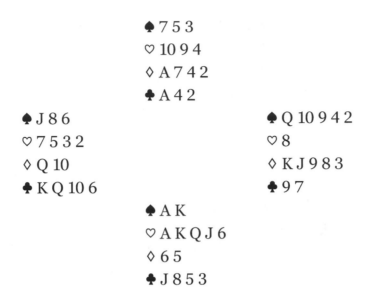

North-South reach 4♡ after a 1-2-4 auction. West led the ♡ 2.

Nine top tricks in notrump, declarer tried for a club ruff. But with the trump lead, he was a step behind. He played the club ace and conceded a club. Back came a trump. He tried again, same result. Down one.

"Partner, seems they always make the right lead against me," said South.
"Seems you always misplay it the same way," thought North.

Could you have found a tenth trick?

The trump lead made life difficult but not impossible. Look at the good trump spots in dummy. What does that suggest? Win the opening lead in hand and cash the ♠AK. When you duck a diamond, West wins and continues a trump.

Win in dummy and ruff a spade. Cross to the ◊A, ruff a diamond, return to the ♣A and ruff the last diamond.

You have taken two high trumps, two high spades, two minor aces, and three ruffs in your hand. That nice ♡9 is sitting in the dummy as the fulfilling trick.

DEAL # 27   TOO EASY

```
              ♠ A K Q 9
              ♡ 6 4 3
              ◊ K 3 2
              ♣ Q 8 6
♠ J 10 5 4                    ♠ void
♡ 8 5                        ♡ J 10 9 7
◊ J 10 9 6                   ◊ A Q 4
♣ K 9 4                      ♣ J 10 7 5 3 2
              ♠ 8 7 6 3 2
              ♡ A K Q 2
              ◊ 8 7 5
              ♣ A
```

North opened 1♣ and South bid 1♠. North raised to 2♠ and South bid 4♠. West led the ◊ J.

The defense took the first three diamond tricks. Then East shifted to a heart. South won and led a trump, getting ready to claim. When East showed out, play slowed.

Declarer led a club to his ace and a second spade. West split his honors. South ruffed a club and drew the trumps. He lost a heart at the end.

Unlucky? The mark of an expert is he doesn't mess up the easy ones.

Simple contracts call for extra care. What could go wrong? It seems like it always does. Declarer must cash the club ace before touching the trumps.

Now after the first round of trumps, South can ruff a club, lead a trump, ruff another club (the key difference), and pick up trumps.

South has four trumps in dummy, one high club, two club ruffs, and three high hearts.

DEAL # 28   COUNT YOUR TRICKS

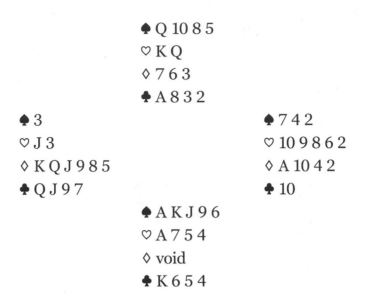

♠ Q 10 8 5
♡ K Q
◊ 7 6 3
♣ A 8 3 2

♠ 3
♡ J 3
◊ K Q J 9 8 5
♣ Q J 9 7

♠ 7 4 2
♡ 10 9 8 6 2
◊ A 10 4 2
♣ 10

♠ A K J 9 6
♡ A 7 5 4
◊ void
♣ K 6 5 4

South opened 1♠, North bis 3♠, a limit raise with four trumps. South considered bidding 5◊, Exclusion Keycard Blackwood, but decided less information might be better. He bid 6♠. West led the ◊ K.

Declarer ruffed the opening lead and drew trumps. When he cashed the ♣AK and East showed out, he realized he only had eleven tricks. Down one.

Was there a way to get twelve tricks? From where?

Count winners, not just losers. With three high hearts and two high diamonds, you need how many trump tricks? Seven. Very good, you can add.

At Trick 2, lead a heart to dummy and ruff another diamond high. Then cross to dummy with a trump and ruff the last diamond high. Now draw trumps.

Four trumps in dummy, three ruffs in hand, three high hearts, and two high **clubs;** you don't have to be a math major.

DEAL # 29   WRONG SUIT

                    ♠ A J 4
                    ♡ A J 10 9
                    ◇ A K J 10
                    ♣ 6 4
    ♠ 9 8   ♠ 6 5 3 2
    ♡ 7 5 3 2   ♡ 6
    ◇ Q 9 7 3   ◇ 8 6 4 2
    ♣ A Q 7   ♣ J 10 9 2
                    ♠ K Q 10 7
                    ♡ K Q 8 4
                    ◇ 5
                    ♣ K 8 5 3

North opened 1◇ and South bid 1♡. How many hearts should North bid? 3? 4? I think North should bid 2NT first. If South passes, so be it. If South bids New Minor, North can bid 4♡. South bid 3♣ which this pair was playing as New Minor. North bid 4♡ and South bid 6♡. West led the ♠ 9.

South bid this hand better than he played it. He won the opening lead in dummy and bet everything on a club finesse. Down one.

How would you have played?

Looking at those good trump spots in dummy, good enough to handle the trump suit, give thought to ruffing in your hand.

Win the opening lead and cash the ◇A. Ruff a diamond with the trump king and lead a trump to dummy. Lead another diamond and ruff with the trump queen. Lead your last trump to dummy.

Draw the last two trumps, discarding clubs from the South hand. Cash the diamond king discarding a club. Cash the rest of the high spades for twelve tricks and lose the last trick to the club ace.

DEAL # 30   BREAKING THE 'RULES'

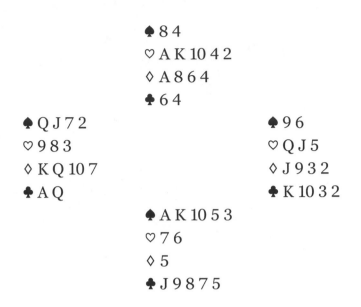

♠ 8 4
♡ A K 10 4 2
♦ A 8 6 4
♣ 6 4

♠ Q J 7 2   ♠ 9 6
♡ 9 8 3   ♡ Q J 5
♦ K Q 10 7   ♦ J 9 3 2
♣ A Q   ♣ K 10 3 2

♠ A K 10 5 3
♡ 7 6
♦ 5
♣ J 9 8 7 5

At favorable vulnerability, South opened an off-beat 2♠. Everyone passed. West led the ♦ K.

Declarer won and started the clubs. West won the ♣Q and shifted to a trump. Declarer won and led another club. West won and played another trump.

Declarer won, cashed two high hearts and ruffed a heart. He had to play the rest out of his hand, An unsuccessful adventure.

What 'rule' should you be breaking?

Usually not ruffing in the hand with the long trumps is a good 'rule' - make that a 'guideline'. But you need to recognize the exceptions.

Take the ♦A at Trick 1 and ruff a diamond. Cash the ♠AK. That's four tricks. Cross to the ♡K and ruff another diamond. That's six tricks. Back to the ♡A and lead another diamond.
Ruff it and when both opponents follow, that's eight tricks.

DEAL # 31   TOO MUCH KNOWLEDGE

<pre>
                        ♠ 10 8 4
                        ♡ A 9 4 3
                        ◇ A Q 3
                        ♣ K 9 7
        ♠ 3   ♠ 9 7 5 2
        ♡ K 8 7 6 2   ♡ J 10 5
        ◇ J 8 6   ◇ 10 9 2
        ♣ J 8 5 2   ♣ Q 10 3
                        ♠ A K Q J 6
                        ♡ Q
                        ◇ K 7 5 4
                        ♣ A 6 4
</pre>

South opened 1♠. North forced to game bidding 2♣. South bid 2◇ and North bid 2♠ promising three pieces. South bid 4♡, a splinter showing extra values with heart shortness. North liked his hand, aces and a king and checked for keycards and the trump queen and reached 6♠. West led the ♠3.

Declarer counted eleven tricks. An extra trick could come from 3-3 diamonds or a dummy reversal. Diamonds was a 35-40% chance, a dummy reversal needing 3-2 trumps about 67%. Declarer decided to go with the odds.

He won the opening lead, led a heart to the ace and ruffed a heart high. Using the ◇AQ as entries, he ruffed two more hearts, embarking on a dummy reversal. When trumps were 4-1, he went down one.

Was this a case of too much knowledge or how would you have played?

Good idea, but instead of committing to a dummy reversal at Trick 2, cash one more high trump at Trick 2. If spades are 3-2, play for a dummy reversal. When you discover the 4-1 split, you can fall back on Plan B, 3-3 diamonds.

Draw trumps and play the hand like a beginner who never heard of a dummy reversal. Cash the three high diamonds. It's a miracle; you made the slam like everyone else in the room.

DEAL # 32   OVERBID? BETTER PLAY IT WELL

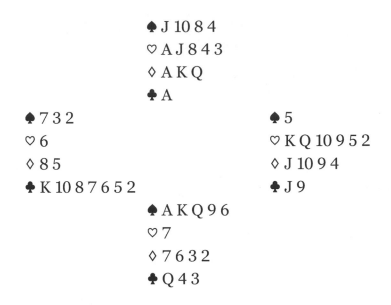

♠ J 10 8 4
♥ A J 8 4 3
♦ A K Q
♣ A

♠ 7 3 2
♥ 6
♦ 8 5
♣ K 10 8 7 6 5 2

♠ 5
♥ K Q 10 9 5 2
♦ J 10 9 4
♣ J 9

♠ A K Q 9 6
♥ 7
♦ 7 6 3 2
♣ Q 4 3

East opened 2♡ and South overcalled 2♠. North blasted to 7♠ after finding partner had the ♠AKQ. West led the ♡ 6.

Declarer won, cashed the ♣A, led a trump to his hand and ruffed a club. He ruffed a heart high and ruffed his last club. He drew trumps and cashed dummy's high diamonds but when East turned up with the ◊J1094, declarer was down one.

Any hope for this ambitious contract?

Yes, of course or it wouldn't be in the book. Win the ♡A and ruff a heart high. Lead a diamond to dummy's ace and ruff a heart high. Cross to dummy with a trump for another heart ruff, then cash the ♣A and ruff another heart.

Now ruff a club and win the rest with the ♠J10 and the ◊KQ.

DEAL # 33   WISHFUL THINKING

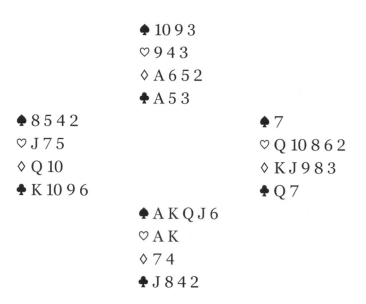

♠ 10 9 3
♥ 9 4 3
♦ A 6 5 2
♣ A 5 3

♠ 8 5 4 2
♥ J 7 5
♦ Q 10
♣ K 10 9 6

♠ 7
♥ Q 10 8 6 2
♦ K J 9 8 3
♣ Q 7

♠ A K Q J 6
♥ A K
♦ 7 4
♣ J 8 4 2

South reaches 4♠ after a 1-2-4 auction. West led the ♠ 2.

Declarer counted nine tricks. If she could ruff a club, that would be ten. But she was behind in the race. She had to lose two clubs and that pesky West kept those trumps coming every time.

Declarer lost three clubs and a diamond, finishing with the same nine tricks she started with.

Where should the tenth trick come from?

Declarer was up-side down. She should have been ruffing in hand, a good example of a dummy reversal even with 4-1 trumps.
Win the first trump in hand, cash the ♡AK and lead a diamond to the ◇A.
Ruff a heart high and concede a diamond.

Win the second trump return in dummy, ruff a diamond high, cross to the ♣A and ruff another diamond. With nine tricks in the bag, there is still a high trump in dummy.

Even the famous Evelyn, Mrs. Ruff-ruff, can make it home from here.

DEAL # 34 A SIMILAR THEME

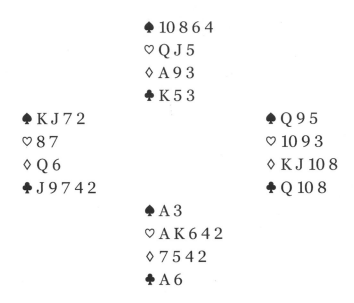

```
              ♠ 10 8 6 4
              ♡ Q J 5
              ◊ A 9 3
              ♣ K 5 3
♠ K J 7 2                    ♠ Q 9 5
♡ 8 7                       ♡ 10 9 3
◊ Q 6                       ◊ K J 10 8
♣ J 9 7 4 2                 ♣ Q 10 8
              ♠ A 3
              ♡ A K 6 4 2
              ◊ 7 5 4 2
              ♣ A 6
```

South opened 1♡. North showed a three-card limit raise and South bid 4♡. West led the ♡7.

The declarer again was the infamous Evelyn who of course had not learned from the previous similar hand. She won the opening lead and tried to ruff a diamond in dummy for a tenth trick.

She cashed the ◊A and ducked a diamond. Back came a trump. Evelyn won and ducked another diamond, but East won and played his last trump. You know the 'rest of the story.'

"Evelyn, we just had a deal like this," moaned Allan, having seen this all too often.

Where would you find your tenth trick?

I know you don't need to review the previous deal to get this one right. Win the opening lead in hand, cash the top clubs and ruff a club. Now cash the ♠A and concede a spade.

Win the trump return in dummy and ruff a spade. Then cross to the ◊A to ruff another spade. Same story- nine in the bag and a good trump in dummy.

Just be glad you don't have to play with Evelyn like I do.

CHAPTER TWO

DEFENSE

Defense to Reversing the Dummy

Similar to defending against a cross-ruff, where leading trumps as often as possible is best, the defenders have little they can do playing against a competent declarer when conditions are right for reversing the dummy.

Sometimes the defense, instead of defending passively by forcing declarer to ruff, may find it beneficial to switch. Declarer may be short entries and by forcing declarer, the defenders are actually helping him ruff a suit he could not do left to his own.

When declarer has plenty of trumps and is not drawing trumps, your level of suspicion as a defender should be high on the alert. Here are two hands to illustrate these points.

DEAL # 35   GOOD DEFENSE

```
                    ♠ 8 6 5 4
                    ♡ K J 2
                    ◊ A J 5
                    ♣ K 5 3
   ♠ A K J 3                        ♠ Q 10 9 2
   ♡ 9 6                            ♡ 10 8 7
   ◊ 10 9 8 3                       ◊ Q 7 6
   ♣ 10 7 4                         ♣ 9 8 2
                    ♠ 7
                    ♡ A Q 5 4 3
                    ◊ K 4 2
                    ♣ A Q J 6
```

North opened 1♣ and South bid 1♡. North raised to 2♡. South bid 3♠, a splinter slam try. North's minimum suddenly became a perfect hand. He bid 4NT, South bid 5♠ and North bid 6♡. West led the ♠ A.

West continued with the ♠K and declarer ruffed. He cashed the ♡A, then the ♡K. When both opponents followed, he ruffed a spade and crossed to the ♣K. Declarer ruffed the last spade with the ♡Q and crossed to dummy with the ◊A.

He drew the last trump with the ♡J, discarding the losing diamond from his hand. Making 6♡.

Do you want to comment on anyone's play?

100% blame to West. If at Trick 2, he does not make the friendly play of helping declarer ruff a spade, the contract is doomed. There are insufficient entries. A trump return at Trick 2 will scuttle the slam.
West should know from the bidding South has a singleton. A trump switch is the only chance to defeat the slam.

DEAL # 36   CAUGHT NAPPING

<pre>
                    ♠ K 6 4
                    ♡ J 7 4
                    ◊ A 7 3
                    ♣ J 9 7 5
    ♠ Q 10 8 3 2   ♠ J 9
    ♡ Q 9 8   ♡ A K 3
    ◊ 8 5   ◊ 4 2
    ♣ K Q 2   ♣ A 10 8 6 4 3
                    ♠ A 7 5
                    ♡ 10 6 5 2
                    ◊ K Q J 10 9 6
                    ♣ void
</pre>

South	West	North	East
1◊	P	1NT	2♣
2◊	3♣	3◊	P
P	4♣	4◊	All Pass

Opening Lead: ♣ K

Declarer ruffed the opening lead and counted only eight sure winners. She led a heart. West won and played another club. Declarer ruffed and led another heart. This time East won and played a third club. Declarer ruffed and led one more heart, finding the hearts 3-3. Another club came back, ruffed by South, her fourth ruff.

At this point, with four tricks in the bag, declarer cashed her last two trumps, the ◊KQ and crossed to the ♠K. She discarded her spade loser on dummy's last trump, came to hand with the ♠A and cashed the good heart for ten tricks.

How could the defense have done better?

The late expert Bernie Chazen called this PPTLF – permanent paralysis of the trump leading finger. At any point, all the opponents had to do was lead a trump. By continuing to force, or tap, the declarer, they were assisting the process of the dummy reversal.

When a declarer is well stocked in trump and isn't drawing them, be alert that maybe you should be leading one yourself.

CHAPTER THREE

ADVANCED
EXAMPLE DEALS

DEAL # 37   DON'T UPPERCUT YOURSELF

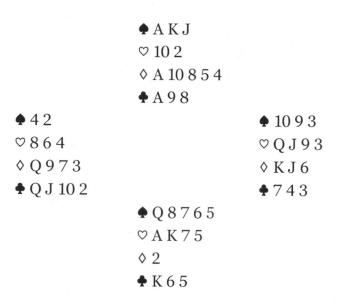

♠ A K J
♥ 10 2
♦ A 10 8 5 4
♣ A 9 8

♠ 4 2
♥ 8 6 4
♦ Q 9 7 3
♣ Q J 10 2

♠ 10 9 3
♥ Q J 9 3
♦ K J 6
♣ 7 4 3

♠ Q 8 7 6 5
♥ A K 7 5
♦ 2
♣ K 6 5

South opened 1♠ and North bid 2♦, game forcing. South bid 2♥ and North bid 2♠. After a few cue bids, North asked for keycards and the trump queen, then settled in 6♠. West led the ♣ Q.

Not seeing the danger on the horizon, declarer won the opening lead in hand and cashed the ♥AK. He ruffed a heart and played the diamond ace. He ruffed a diamond and ruffed his last heart loser.

When he drew trump, he now saw what he had done to himself. East now had a trump trick. With a late club loser, declarer was down one.

Ruffing yes, but ruffing what? Don't promote a trick for the opponents.

Win the opening lead and cash the ace of diamonds. Now a diamond ruff, cross to dummy with a trump and ruff another diamond. A club to the ace and a third diamond ruff means twelve tricks for the good guys.

DEAL # 38   HOPE FOR THE BEST

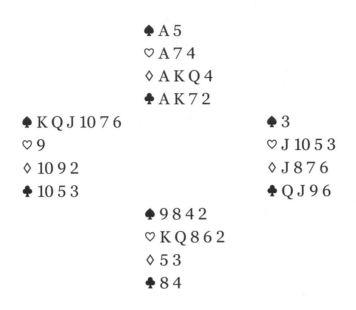

       ♠ A 5
       ♡ A 7 4
       ◊ A K Q 4
       ♣ A K 7 2

♠ K Q J 10 7 6   ♠ 3
♡ 9   ♡ J 10 5 3
◊ 10 9 2   ◊ J 8 7 6
♣ 10 5 3   ♣ Q J 9 6

       ♠ 9 8 4 2
       ♡ K Q 8 6 2
       ◊ 5 3
       ♣ 8 4

North opened 2♣ and South bid 2◊, a waiting bid. West bid 2♠ and North doubled for take-out. When South bid 4♡, North bid 6♡. West led the ♠ K.

Declarer started with eleven tricks. He attempted to ruff a spade in dummy, which from the bidding was unlikely to succeed. Down one.

Do you see any hope for this poor contract?

Maybe. If East has length in the minors, at least 4-4, there is a possible line of play. Win the opening lead and lead a heart to the king. Cash the heart queen.

Cash the ♣AK and ruff a club. Cross to the ◊A and ruff the last club. A diamond to dummy's king, cash the diamond queen and ruff the last diamond.

That's eleven tricks and dummy still has the ace of trumps for twelve.

DEAL # 39   THE MISSING TENTH TRICK

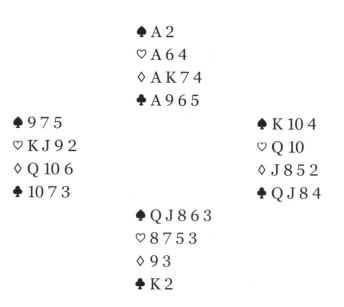

North opened 1♣ and South bid 1♠. When North rebid 2NT, South bid 4♠. West led the ♠5.

Declarer took the spade finesse at Trick 1. East won the king and returned a trump. Declarer played a club to his king and drew the last trump. He finished with nine tricks.

Down one. "Finesses, finesses," moaned North.

Where is the tenth trick lurking? Is there one?

There is if you refuse the finesse at Trick 1. What you can't afford is a second trump play. Win the ♠A at Trick 1. Play the king, then ace of clubs and ruff a club. Cross to dummy with a diamond and ruffed the last club high.

Again, over to dummy with a diamond and ruff a diamond. Now finally a heart to the ace and ruff the last diamond with South's last trump.

How many tricks have you taken at this point? One trump (Trick 1), one high heart, two high clubs, two high diamonds, and four ruffs in the South hand.

Can you add that up?

DEAL # 40   MULTIPLE CHOICES

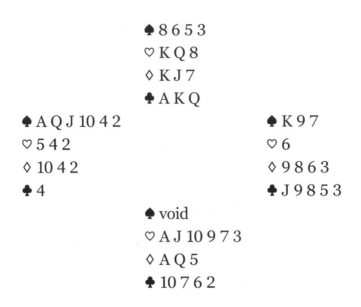

♠ 8 6 5 3
♡ K Q 8
♢ K J 7
♣ A K Q

♠ A Q J 10 4 2   ♠ K 9 7
♡ 5 4 2   ♡ 6
♢ 10 4 2   ♢ 9 8 6 3
♣ 4   ♣ J 9 8 5 3

♠ void
♡ A J 10 9 7 3
♢ A Q 5
♣ 10 7 6 2

South opened 1♡. West overcalled 2♠ and North bid 3♠ showing a game force with hearts. East doubled to show a spade honor and South redoubled, showing a spade control. North bid 4NT. South bid 5NT, two keycards and a void. North bid 7♡. West led a trump.

South saw two possible lines of play. If trumps were 2-2, he could ruff a club. Otherwise, if clubs were 3-3, he had thirteen tricks. He cashed a second round of trumps, then tried line two. Down one.

Was there another door to open?

Declarer can combine his chances by trying for a dummy reversal while testing trumps. Win Trick 1 in dummy and ruff a spade high. A low trump to dummy reveals the 3-1 split so ruff another spade. A club to dummy and another spade ruff. Then a diamond to dummy followed by ruffing the last spade.

How to get back to dummy? With more diamonds out than clubs, diamonds are safer. A diamond to dummy, draw the last trump discarding the club loser. Thirteen tricks: four spade ruffs, three trump tricks, three diamond tricks, and three club tricks.

DEAL # 41   EXTRA RISK

```
              ♠ J 10 9
              ♡ A K 5
              ◊ A 7 5 4
              ♣ Q 5 4
♠ 8 4 3                        ♠ 6 2
♡ Q J 10                       ♡ 8 7 6 2
◊ K J 10 9                     ◊ Q 6 3 2
♣ 7 3 2                        ♣ 10 9 8
              ♠ A K Q 7 5
              ♡ 9 4 3
              ◊ 8
              ♣ A K J 6
```

South opened 1♠ and North bid 2♣ creating a game force. South's 3◊ bid was a splinter raise of clubs and North bid 3♠. After two cue bids, South bid 4NT. When North showed two aces, South bid 5NT. North showed the heart king and South bid 7♠. West led a trump.

Declarer saw his only chance was one hand with four clubs and three trumps. He drew two rounds of trump, and tried to play four rounds of clubs to discard a heart from dummy. Down one.

Do you see a more likely successful line of play?

Probably. Win the trump lead in dummy and cash the ◊A. Ruff a diamond high and cross to dummy with a low trump. Ruff another diamond high and go to dummy with a top heart. Ruff the last diamond with South's last trump.

Cross to the remaining high heart in dummy. Draw the outstanding trumps, discarding South's heart loser.

Thirteen tricks: Three trumps, four clubs, three red suit winners, and three diamond ruffs. These are the kind of grand slams where in a team game you often compare and find they were only in game at the other table. A small slam would have won almost as many IMP's with much less risk.

DEAL # 42   AN EXOTIC TRY

```
                    ♠ 8 6 3
                    ♡ K J 9
                    ◊ A 4 2
                    ♣ A 9 6 3
   ♠ 2                            ♠ K J 10 9 4
   ♡ 8 6 3                        ♡ 7 4
   ◊ Q 10 8 7 5                   ◊ K 6
   ♣ J 8 4 2                      ♣ K Q 10 7
                    ♠ A Q 7 5
                    ♡ A Q 10 5 2
                    ◊ J 9 3
                    ♣ 5
```

East bid 1♠. South overcalled 2♡. North's cue bid showed a good hand with hearts. South bid 4♡, his spade honors being well placed. West led the ♠ 2.

Declarer was looking at nine tricks, the ♠AQ, five trumps and two minor aces. Declarer drew trumps and crossed to the ♣A. He led the ◊2. If East had ◊K10 or ◊Q10, declarer planned to cover the ten and later drop East's remaining honor.

The ◊9 would be his tenth trick.

Thoughtful, but unsuccessful. Anything better?

If trumps are 3-2, better odds than the above position, three diamond ruffs in the South hand will yield an extra trump trick.

At Trick 2, cross to the ♣A and ruff a club high. Lead a low trump to the nine and ruff another club high. A low trump to dummy's jack and a final club ruff high completes the job. Now simply cross to the ◊A and draw the last trump.

Two high spades, two minor aces, three club ruffs, and three trumps in dummy means ten tricks.

DEAL # 43   ANNOYING LEAD

```
                          ♠ A J 8
                          ♡ A Q 7
                          ◇ A J 8 5
                          ♣ 10 3 2
        ♠ 6 4 3 2                          ♠ 10 9 5
        ♡ 8 6                              ♡ 10 9 2
        ◇ 10 6 4                           ◇ K 9 7 3 2
        ♣ A J 8 7                          ♣ K 9
                          ♠ K Q 7
                          ♡ K J 5 4 3
                          ◇ Q
                          ♣ Q 6 5 4
```

South opened 1♡ and North first bid 2♦, game forcing, then supported hearts. North had visions of big things but South signed off in 4♡. West led a trump.

With a different lead, South might have had time to start clubs, perhaps ruffing the fourth club. He drew the rest of the trumps and tried to play the club suit himself. Down one.

How would you have played the club suit?

Trick question. I hope you answered, "Not at all." Instead, win the opening lead in hand and lead a diamond to the ace, please, no finesse. Ruff a diamond and cross back to dummy with the trump queen.

Ruff another diamond and back to dummy with the spade jack. Ruff the last diamond and return to dummy with the spade ace. Draw the last trump, discarding a club.

The defenders collect three club tricks, declarer has the rest.

DEAL # 44   THE 4/3 FIT

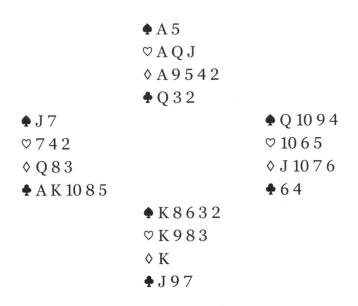

♠ A 5
♡ A Q J
♢ A 9 5 4 2
♣ Q 3 2

♠ J 7
♡ 7 4 2
♢ Q 8 3
♣ A K 10 8 5

♠ Q 10 9 4
♡ 10 6 5
♢ J 10 7 6
♣ 6 4

♠ K 8 6 3 2
♡ K 9 8 3
♢ K
♣ J 9 7

North opened 1NT and the bidding got a bit off track. South transferred to spades and bid hearts. He ended in 4♡ in a 4-3 heart fit. West led the ♣AK and another club which East ruffed. East returned the ♢J.

Declarer tried ruffing a spade in dummy which needed a 3-3 split. He finished down one. Poorly bid, poorly played.

How would you have played if you got yourself in this contract?

Win the diamond return with the king, cross to dummy with a trump and ruff a small diamond. Then back to dummy with another trump and ruff another diamond with the ♡K. Then a spade to the ace, draw a third round of trumps clearing the suit.

Cash the diamonds and a spade to the king. Ten tricks.

DEAL # 45   ANOTHER 4/3 FIT

```
                    ♠ A K 4
                    ♡ J 8 5 3
                    ◊ A 10 3
                    ♣ 10 9 4
      ♠ Q J 5                        ♠ 9 7 2
      ♡ K Q 10 6                     ♡ A 9 7 4
      ◊ 9 5                          ◊ 8 6 4
      ♣ K Q 7 5                      ♣ J 6 2
                    ♠ 10 8 6 3
                    ♡ 2
                    ◊ K Q J 7 2
                    ♣ A 8 3
```

West opened 1♣ and North made a marginal take-out double. East passed and South with a good hand cue bid 2♣. North bid 2♡ and South bid 2♠. Should North bid 2NT? He raised to 3♠ and South bid 4♠. West led the ♡ K.

Declarer did not have ten tricks. He played the ♠AK and a third spade. Trumps were 3-3 but declarer only had nine tricks. Down one. Imagine if trumps were 4-2.

How would you handle this contract? 4-3 fits are always difficult.

Ruff the second heart and cross to the ace of spades. Ruff another heart and cross to the ace of diamonds. Ruff your last heart. Whew, hearts are 4-4, one hurdle cleared.

Now a diamond to the ten and cash the king of spades. Lead your last trump and hope for a 3-3 break. Yes! And West is in with nothing but clubs. Take your ace and run the diamonds.

South finishes with two high spades in dummy, three heart ruffs in hand, the ace of clubs, and five diamonds. Where did all these tricks come from?

West asks East, "Did you have the jack of clubs? I could have beaten the contract with a club shift at Trick 2!"

53

DEAL # 46   LOT TO DO

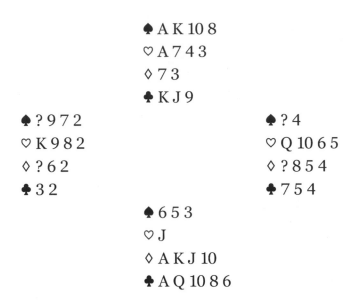

♠ A K 10 8
♥ A 7 4 3
♦ 7 3
♣ K J 9

♠ ? 9 7 2
♥ K 9 8 2
♦ ? 6 2
♣ 3 2

♠ ? 4
♥ Q 10 6 5
♦ ? 8 5 4
♣ 7 5 4

♠ 6 5 3
♥ J
♦ A K J 10
♣ A Q 10 8 6

South opened 1♣ and reversed into 2♦. After that start, North propelled the partnership into 7♣. An ambitious contract, but he didn't have to play it, South did. West led the ♣ 2.

So many choices. Finesses, dummy reversal, where to start? Declarer won the opening lead in dummy and cashed the heart ace. He ruffed three hearts in hand using one trump and the ♠AK as entries. Then he drew the last trump in dummy, discarding his spade loser and took a successful diamond finesse.

But with no trump left, he cashed the ♦AK and the ♦Q did not drop. Down one.

Do you see any way around the problem?

Declarer was on the right track but just slipped a hair. Entry problems, and often they are seen too late as is the case here. If you take a diamond finesse at Trick 2 (yes, I know, no one likes to go down at Trick 2), then continue as above, you can repeat the diamond finesse at the end.

DEAL # 47   CHANGING LANES

$\spadesuit$ Q J 4
$\heartsuit$ A Q 8 2
$\diamond$ K 5
$\clubsuit$ A 8 7 4

$\spadesuit$ 8 $\spadesuit$ 9 6 3 2
$\heartsuit$ K J 9 5 4 $\heartsuit$ 10 7
$\diamond$ 10 4 3 2 $\diamond$ 9 7
$\clubsuit$ J 10 9 $\clubsuit$ K Q 6 3 2

$\spadesuit$ A K 10 7 5
$\heartsuit$ 6 3
$\diamond$ A Q J 8 6
$\clubsuit$ 5

South opened 1$\spadesuit$ and North bid 2$\clubsuit$, game forcing. South bid 2$\diamond$, North bid 2$\spadesuit$. When South bid 3$\diamond$, North checked for keycards and drove to 7$\spadesuit$. West led the $\clubsuit$ J.

South won the $\clubsuit$A and counted twelve tricks. Having just read a book on Reversing the Dummy, he ruffed a club at Trick 2, his first good play. He cashed the $\spadesuit$A, his second good play.

To ruff another club, he crossed to dummy with the $\diamond$K, his fatal play. When he ruffed another club, he lost control of the hand since trumps were 4-1.

What is one of the requirements for a successful dummy reversal?

Almost always, trumps need be 3-2. Rather than cross to the $\diamond$K, declarer should cross in trumps. If trumps are 3-2, he can proceed with the dummy reversal.

But when he discovers the 4-1 split, he still has time to abandon this line, draw trumps and take the heart finesse.

DEAL # 48   THANKS FOR THE NINE

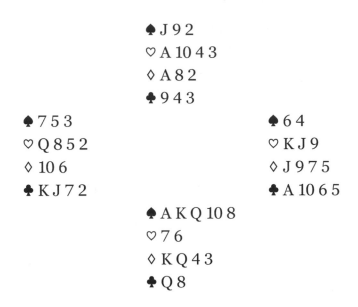

  ♠ J 9 2
  ♡ A 10 4 3
  ◇ A 8 2
  ♣ 9 4 3

♠ 7 5 3   ♠ 6 4
♡ Q 8 5 2   ♡ K J 9
◇ 10 6   ◇ J 9 7 5
♣ K J 7 2   ♣ A 10 6 5

  ♠ A K Q 10 8
  ♡ 7 6
  ◇ K Q 4 3
  ♣ Q 8

South opened 1♠. When North bid 2♠, South made a game try bidding 3◇. North bid 4♠. West led the ♣ 2.

East won the ♣A and returned a club to West's ♣K. South ruffed the third club. Declarer drew two rounds of trump and tested the diamonds. If diamonds were 3-3, or if the opponent with four diamonds didn't have the last trump, he would be OK. Not in this book. Down one.

How should you play (in this book)?

First, get into the habit of not ruffing with your lowest trump if possible. Ruff Trick 3 with your ten. (Can't you hear Eddie saying "Carefully preserved is carefully preserved)? Duck a heart at Trick 4, saving the ♡A as an entry.

Their best return is a trump. Win in your hand (high!), cross to the ♡A and ruff a heart. You are left with a high trump and the ♠8. Cross to the ◇A and ruff dummy's last heart high. OK, now you can play your ♠8 to dummy's nine. Draw the last trump with dummy's jack, discarding a diamond.

Be sure to thank North for the spade nine. If dummy had ♠J32, you would have been short one entry.

DEAL # 49   DECLARE OR DEFEND?

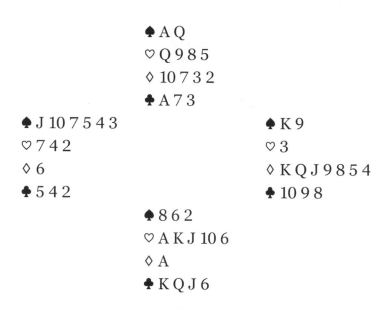

```
              ♠ A Q
              ♡ Q 9 8 5
              ◊ 10 7 3 2
              ♣ A 7 3
♠ J 10 7 5 4 3              ♠ K 9
♡ 7 4 2                    ♡ 3
◊ 6                        ◊ K Q J 9 8 5 4
♣ 5 4 2                    ♣ 10 9 8
              ♠ 8 6 2
              ♡ A K J 10 6
              ◊ A
              ♣ K Q J 6
```

South opened 1♡ and North bid 2NT, conventionally a forcing heart raise. East bid 3◊ and South doubled, showing a diamond control. When North cue bid 3♠, South checked for keycards and bid 7♡. West led ◊ 6.

Declarer won the opening lead and drew trumps. Never one to pass up a finesse, he led a spade to the queen. Down one.

Would you have taken the finesse? Do you want to declare or defend?

I hope not. Win the opening lead and cross to dummy's ♡8. Ruff a diamond high and lead the ♡10 to the ♡Q. Ruff another diamond high and lead a club to the ace. Ruff the last diamond.

Lead a spade to the ace and draw the last trump, discarding a spade. Cash the clubs, discarding the ♠Q on the last club. Ruff your last spade.

Which did you choose? I chose to defend and led a trump, taking out an entry before declarer could start the dummy reversal. Down one.

DEAL # 50   PLAN_AHEAD

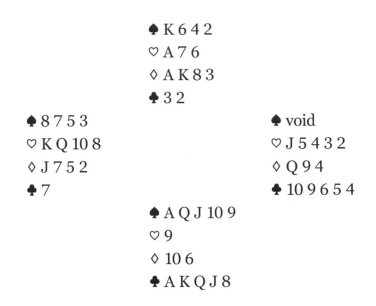

♠ K 6 4 2
♡ A 7 6
◊ A K 8 3
♣ 3 2

♠ 8 7 5 3
♡ K Q 10 8
◊ J 7 5 2
♣ 7

♠ void
♡ J 5 4 3 2
◊ Q 9 4
♣ 10 9 6 5 4

♠ A Q J 10 9
♡ 9
◊ 10 6
♣ A K Q J 8

South opened 1♠ and North bid 2NT, a conventional forcing spade raise. South bid 4♣, natural, a second good suit, a source of tricks. After North cue bid 4◊, South checked for keycards. North responded 5◊, none (very unlikely) or three. South bid 5NT, specific king asking, and North bid 6◊, the ◊K. South bid 7♠. West led the ♡ K.

Declarer won the ace and led a spade. East showed out. OK, he thought. it's unlikely to matter. He drew four rounds of trumps and started the clubs. When West showed on the second club, declarer was down one. No club ruff in dummy.

Could this Greek tragedy have been avoided?

In a grand slam, you better be on your toes, thinking "What could go wrong?" To counter a 4-0 trump break, ruff a heart at Trick 2. Now you can cash the ♠A. When East shows out, go to dummy with the ◊A and ruff another heart.

Cash the last two trumps in your hand and cross to dummy with another high diamond. Draw the last trump with dummy's ♠K, discarding the fifth club.
One heart, two heart ruffs, four spades, two diamonds, and four clubs.

Isn't that just Grand?

DEAL # 51   TWO WAYS HOME

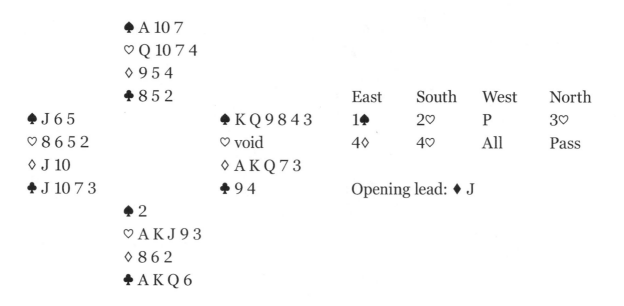

```
                    ♠ A 10 7
                    ♡ Q 10 7 4
                    ◇ 9 5 4
                    ♣ 8 5 2                    East    South    West    North
♠ J 6 5                        ♠ K Q 9 8 4 3   1♠      2♡       P       3♡
♡ 8 6 5 2                      ♡ void          4◇      4♡       All     Pass
◇ J 10                         ◇ A K Q 7 3
♣ J 10 7 3                     ♣ 9 4           Opening lead: ◆ J
                    ♠ 2
                    ♡ A K J 9 3
                    ◇ 8 6 2
                    ♣ A K Q 6
```

East won the first three diamond tricks, West discarding a spade on the third diamond. East switched to the ♠K. Declarer won the ♠A and led a heart.

When East showed out, declarer drew four rounds of trumps. He then started the clubs but when they divided 4-2, he was down one.

What should declarer have done with his fourth club?

He actually had two choices. From the bidding, East could not have more than three clubs, and likely even less. Before drawing trumps, you can play three rounds of clubs and ruff a club if necessary.

A more elegant way, now that you are a Dummy Reversal Expert, is to ruff a spade at Trick 5 in hand with the ♡A. Then play the ♡K and a heart to dummy.

Ruff the last spade with a high heart. Lead a low heart to dummy and finish the trumps, discarding your low club. Sit back and wait for the applause.

DEAL # 52   A DECLARER REVERSAL

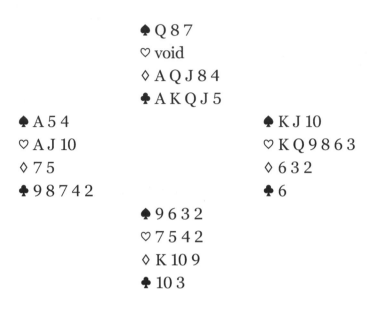

```
                    ♠ Q 8 7
                    ♡ void
                    ◊ A Q J 8 4
                    ♣ A K Q J 5
   ♠ A 5 4                          ♠ K J 10
   ♡ A J 10                         ♡ K Q 9 8 6 3
   ◊ 7 5                            ◊ 6 3 2
   ♣ 9 8 7 4 2                      ♣ 6
                    ♠ 9 6 3 2
                    ♡ 7 5 4 2
                    ◊ K 10 9
                    ♣ 10 3
```

East opened 2♡ and West raised to 4♡. North bid 4NT for the minors. South bid 5◊. West led the ♡ A.

(I think if you are going to lead an ace on this auction, I'd lead the ♠A, less likely to be ruffed. Here E/W would take the first three spade tricks).

Declarer ruffed the opening heart lead and drew trumps. He ran his clubs and diamonds, finishing with the same ten tricks he started with. Down one.

Where oh where is there an eleventh trick?

For once it's right to do the natural thing – start ruffing. Ruff the opening lead. Cross to your hand with a diamond and ruff another heart. Cross again to your hand with a diamond and ruff another heart with dummy's last trump.

Come back to your hand with the ten of clubs and play your last diamond, discarding a spade. If diamonds are 3-2, you are making five diamonds.

Sort of a declarer reversal, no? Good thing West didn't lead a spade.

DEAL # 53   MAKING USE OF YOUR TRUMPS

```
                    ♠ K 8
                    ♡ A 5 4 3
                    ◊ 8 7 5 3
                    ♣ A K 5
   ♠ Q                              ♠ J 10 7 4
   ♡ Q 10 9 6                       ♡ K J 8 2
   ◊ Q J 10 6                       ◊ K 9
   ♣ 10 6 4 2                       ♣ J 8 7
                    ♠ A 9 6 5 3 2
                    ♡ 7
                    ◊ A 4 2
                    ♣ Q 9 3
```

South opened 2♠ and North raised to 4♠. West led the ◊ Q.

Declarer won and played a spade to the king and a spade to the ace. If trumps were 3-2, he had ten tricks. But West showed out on the second round. Declarer could not avoid the loss of two trumps and two diamonds. Down one.

Could you overcome the 4-1 split?

Maybe. After winning the opening lead, it's just good practice to play a heart to the ace and ruff a heart. Look what a difference this makes.

Start trumps by playing the ace, then the king. West shows out. Now ruff another heart. You have the ♠96 left, East has the ♠J10

Cash three rounds of clubs ending in the dummy. OK, a little lucky but you are entitled to some luck too. You have taken nine tricks. Lead a heart. If East ruffs, you outnumber his trumps. If he discards, you ruff.
You have to score a tenth trick Thanks to your early anticipation by ruffing a heart at Trick 2.

Like a trump coup along with a dummy reversal. Very nice!

CROSSRUFFING – DUMMY REVERSAL'S COUSIN

Ruffing in the dummy is common and up to now this book has covered reversing the dummy. Let's just finish with a cousin of this, the crossruff, ruffing in both hands. This works when both hands are short in different side suits, allowing declarer to make more tricks by ruffing out those suits, scoring the trumps separately than by drawing the trumps.

Usually, it does not profit declarer to use his own trumps to ruff losers from the dummy. The idea behind the ruff is to score a trick with a trump which would otherwise be useless. When declarer has solid trumps in his hand, ruffing with these does not produce an extra winner as he can by ruffing with dummy's trumps.

There are hands where to make the contract, declarer must score separately the trumps in dummy and in his hand. This is where the CROSSRUFF takes center stage.

A crossruff is indicated when declarer, after counting his high card winners and number of ruffs, reaches the number of tricks necessary to make his contract. When playing a crossruff, one counts winners rather than losers. It is always important to cash side suit winners early.

The reason is that while you are crossruffing, an opponent may run out of the suit being ruffed and discard from a suit you hold the AK. He may be able to discard and later ruff your AK. Very annoying!

Characteristics of a Good Crossruffing Hand

Different Side Suit Shortness in Both Hands- Ideally opposing singletons (or doubletons), with the other hand having length.

Trump Length- Ideally trumps are split evenly, 4-4, 4-5, etc. When 6-3 or 5-3, standard ruffing techniques are usually best, ruffing in the short side.

Trump Strength- Trump strength prevents overruffing by the opponents.

Top Tricks in the Side Suits-Hands with aces and ace-kings are best, that can be cashed before embarking on the crossruff.

Best Defense- Repeated trump leads, including the opening lead if possible.

Here is a typical example:

West is declarer in 4♡

West	East
♠ 8 6 5 3	♠ 4
♡ A K 10 7 2	♡ Q J 9 8 3
♢ 8	♢ A 7 5 3 2
♣ K 6 5	♣ A 3

In this deal, drawing trumps would leave declarer with spade and club losers in the main hand without a good side suit to discard them on. Instead, establish a crossruff of spades/clubs in the East hand and diamonds in the West hand.

Once you lose the first spade, cash all your side suit winners and start ruffing spades/clubs in the East hand versus diamonds in the West hand. Even if the opponents run out of a suit before you, their trumps are not high enough to be of a concern.

Let's Look at some more example deals:

♠ AJ98   ♠ KQ107   The ♣K is led against your 4♠ contract. If you win the ♣A and
♡ 852   ♡ 943   draw three rounds of trumps, you will take three trumps, two
◇ 8   ◇ A9632   side aces, and one ruff in each hand for seven tricks. If instead,
♣ A9732   ♣ 4   you cash the ♣A, the ◇A and ruff back and forth in the minors
                     without ever touching trumps, you will take ten tricks.

♠ A964   ♠ 2   South leads the ♠K against East's 5◇. The ♠ and ♣ holdings
♡ KJ43   ♡ 75   are classic signs a crossruff may succeed. Strong trumps? Just
◇ KJ54   ◇ AQ763   barely. A 4-4 spade split is needed too. Win the ♠A, cash the ♣A
♣ 8   ♣ A9542   and ruff a club, ruff a spade, continue the crossruff. Start the
                     suit in which you have the greater number of losers.

♠ AKJ98   ♠ Q1076   North leads the ♡Q against West's 6♠. All the trumps are high
♡ A9753   ♡ 4   and four small hearts can be ruffed in the East. Before starting
◇ K97   ◇ A64   the crossruff, cash the ◇AK to avoid having them ruffed later.
♣ void   ♣ 97642   The club ruffs provide transportation to the West hand. A
                     trump lead would hold declarer to one less trick.

DEAL # 54   AN EASIER ROAD HOME

```
                  ♠ A 6
                  ♡ J 8 6 4 3
                  ◊ 7 3
                  ♣ A 7 4 2
♠ 2                               ♠ J 10 9 8 7
♡ Q 10 7 5 2                      ♡ K 9
◊ K 10 9 8                        ◊ A Q
♣ K 6 3                           ♣ J 10 9 5
                  ♠ K Q 5 4 3
                  ♡ A
                  ◊ J 6 5 4 2
                  ♣ Q 8
```

South opened 1♠ and North bid 1NT, forcing for one round. South rebid 2◊ and North took a preference to 2♠. West led the ♣ 3.

A friendly lead for declarer. This looked like a second suit hand. Declarer had just read a book about searching for a second suit so he started the diamonds.

That didn't work very well; he was sorry he had read that book. He finished down two.

Was there another book you prefer?

Try this line of play instead. After winning the ♣Q, lead a club to the ace and ruff a club. Cash the ♡A and cross to dummy with the ♠A. Ruff a heart.

Count your tricks. Three top spades, two clubs, the heart ace, and two ruffs in hand.

Let's see, that's, well what do you know? Eight tricks. I like this book better.

DEAL # 55   GLAD I BID

```
                    ♠ A K Q 3
                    ♡ A 4 3
                    ◊ 5 4
                    ♣ A J 8 2
     ♠ 9 6 5 4                        ♠ 2
     ♡ K Q 10                         ♡ J 9 8 6
     ◊ K J 8                          ◊ Q 10 6
     ♣ Q 6 5                          ♣ K 10 9 7 3
                    ♠ J 10 8 7
                    ♡ 7 5 2
                    ◊ A 9 7 3 2
                    ♣ 4
```

North opened 1♣ and South bid 1♠. North bid 4♠ as South was thinking "Maybe I shouldn't have bid." West led the ♡K.

Declarer won the opening lead and drew two rounds of trumps. When East showed out, he started to do the thinking he should have done two tricks earlier.
He played the ◊A and a small diamond. West won and led another trump.

Declarer finished with one ruff in each hand, three trump tricks, and three aces.
North thought to herself, "Partner, if you are going to play like that, you better not bid with those hands."

Could you have justified your bidding?

"What kind of hand type is this?" you should be asking yourself before starting play. You have no tricks but maybe you can score a lot of trump tricks separately.

Well yes, but not if you draw the trumps. Win the opening lead and cash the ♣A. Ruff a club in hand. Lead the ◊A and another diamond. The defenders will win and cash two heart tricks. Then almost certainly they will return a trump.

You can crossruff the rest of the hand, making exactly ten tricks. South made a good 1♠ bid; he just had to play it better.

66

DEAL # 56   PLAN B

```
                        ♠ A 8 6 2
                        ♡ A 8 7 3
                        ◊ void
                        ♣ A 9 7 4 3
        ♠ Q                                   ♠ K 10 9 3
        ♡ 10 9 6 4                            ♡ K Q 5 2
        ◊ K Q 6 5 2                           ◊ 10 9 8 4
        ♣ K Q J                               ♣ 10
                        ♠ J 7 5 4
                        ♡ J
                        ◊ A J 7 3
                        ♣ 8 6 5 2
```

West opened 1◊ and North made a take-out double. East bid 1♡ and South bid 1♠. West bid 2♡ but North, in love with her aces and a void, raised to 4♠. West led the ♣ K.

Declarer saw a second suit, clubs and decided to draw trumps. He won the opening lead and cashed the ♠A. Then he led a low spade. East won and played a third spade. With no source of tricks, the contract was doomed.

Was there a better plan?

Declarer should have fallen in love with North's aces too. With shortage in both hands, what kind of hand is this? Easy question since we are discussing crossruffs but this has all the hallmarks of a classic crossruff. Lots of quick winners, singletons, lots of trumps.

Take Trick 1 in dummy and cash the ♡A. Ruff a heart and cash the ◊A. Now back and forth for the first nine tricks, ruffing away your losers and you still have the trump ace in dummy for your tenth trick.

DEAL # 57   PLAN AHEAD

$\spadesuit$ A 10 6
$\heartsuit$ 9 8 3 2
$\diamond$ A 9 6 3
$\clubsuit$ 9 5

$\spadesuit$ 4 $\spadesuit$ 8 7 5 3
$\heartsuit$ A K J 10 6 $\heartsuit$ 7 4
$\diamond$ 8 4 2 $\diamond$ Q J 10 7
$\clubsuit$ K J 10 3 $\clubsuit$ 6 4 2

$\spadesuit$ K Q J 9 2
$\heartsuit$ Q 5
$\diamond$ K 5
$\clubsuit$ A Q 8 7

South opened 1$\spadesuit$ and reached 4$\spadesuit$ after West's 2$\heartsuit$ overcall. West led the $\heartsuit$ A.

West continued with the heart king and the jack. Declarer ruffed as East discarded a club. Declarer crossed to dummy with a diamond to take a club finesse. West won and played another high heart.

Declarer ruffed again as East discarded his last club. Declarer tried to cash the $\clubsuit$A but East ruffed.

Down one.

How would you have handled this contract?

Plan ahead and count your tricks. After ruffing the third heart, simply cash your winners; the $\clubsuit$A and the $\diamond$AK.

After conceding a club and winning the trump return, you can crossruff the rest for ten tricks.

DEAL # 58   BETTER TIMING

```
                    ♠ K Q 7
                    ♡ 5
                    ◇ A K 10 2
                    ♣ 10 8 4 3 2
♠ J 9 6 4 2                          ♠ A 10
♡ Q 8 6 4 2                          ♡ 10 9
◇ void                               ◇ 7 6 5 3
♣ Q 6 5                              ♣ A K J 9 7
                    ♠ 8 5 3
                    ♡ A K J 7 3
                    ◇ Q J 9 8 4
                    ♣ void
```

East opened 1♣ and South overcalled 2NT showing the red suits. North liked his hand and cue bid 3♣. South bid 4◇ and North raised to 5◇. West looked everywhere for a trump to lead but finally led the ♣ 5.

Declarer ruffed the opening lead. He cashed the ♡AK and ruffed a heart with the ten of trumps as East discarded the ten of spades.

Declarer continued with three club ruffs in hand and two more heart ruffs with high trumps in dummy. But he finished with ten tricks as East remained with the spade ace and trumps. Down one.

Was there a road to eleven tricks?

At Trick 2, declarer must lead a spade to the king. East will win and lead a trump, but declarer can win the queen and cash the spade queen.

Play proceeds the same but the spade queen plus eight trump tricks plus two top hearts add up to eleven.

DEAL # 59   COUNT EARLY

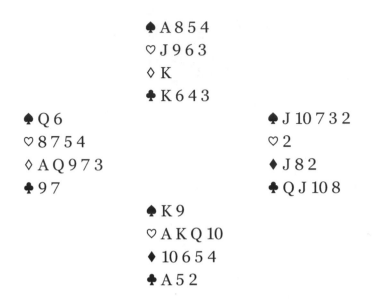

♠ A 8 5 4
♡ J 9 6 3
♢ K
♣ K 6 4 3

♠ Q 6
♡ 8 7 5 4
♢ A Q 9 7 3
♣ 9 7

♠ J 10 7 3 2
♡ 2
♢ J 8 2
♣ Q J 10 8

♠ K 9
♡ A K Q 10
♢ 10 6 5 4
♣ A 5 2

South opened 1NT and reached 4♡ after a Stayman auction. West led the ♡ 4.

Declarer won the opening lead and played a second round of trumps. When East showed out, play slowed as declarer belatedly counted his tricks. Eight on top plus two diamond ruffs, or either black suit breaking 3-3 would be ten tricks.

He led a diamond. West won and led another trump. Eight on top plus one diamond ruff plus nothing else meant down one.

Good defense by West, but how should declarer have played?

Maybe by counting his tricks a bit sooner? After winning the opening lead, duck a diamond. Now you are a step ahead and can ruff two diamonds in the dummy despite that obnoxious Wests' good defense.

Ten tricks means making four hearts.

DEAL # 60　CASH YOUR WINNERS

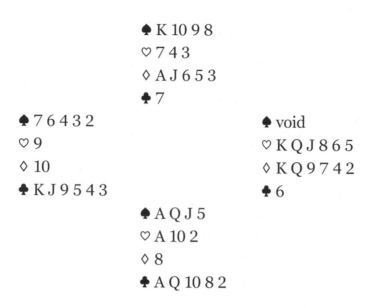

♠ K 10 9 8
♥ 7 4 3
♦ A J 6 5 3
♣ 7

♠ 7 6 4 3 2
♥ 9
♦ 10
♣ K J 9 5 4 3

♠ void
♥ K Q J 8 6 5
♦ K Q 9 7 4 2
♣ 6

♠ A Q J 5
♥ A 10 2
♦ 8
♣ A Q 10 8 2

South opened 1♣ and North bid 1♦. East overcalled 2♥. South bid 2♠ and North raised to 3♠. East bid 4♦, natural. South's 4♠ bid ended the auction. West led the ♠ 2.

Declarer, to counter this diabolical lead, counted ten tricks: three aces and seven trump tricks on a crossruff. He won the spade eight, cashed the ♣A and ruffed a club. When he cashed the ♦A and ruffed a diamond, West discarded a heart. Declarer was toast. Eventually declarer's heart ace was ruffed. Down one.

What basic principle did declarer overlook?

Yes, the lead was diabolical but so was declarer's play. He overlooked the basic principle of cashing as many winners as possible before embarking on his crossruff. This will prevent exactly what happened. Declarer must not allow a defender the opportunity to discard during the crossruff and be able to ruff one of declarer's winners.

If declarer cashes his three aces starting at Trick 2, he can proceed with scoring seven trump tricks and bring this contract home.

DEAL # 61   COUNT YOUR TRICKS

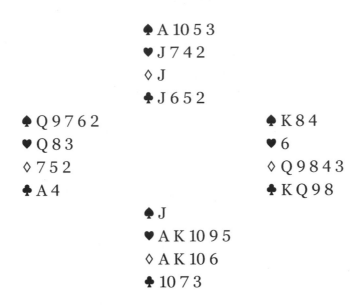

♠ A 10 5 3
♥ J 7 4 2
♦ J
♣ J 6 5 2

♠ Q 9 7 6 2
♥ Q 8 3
♦ 7 5 2
♣ A 4

♠ K 8 4
♥ 6
♦ Q 9 8 4 3
♣ K Q 9 8

♠ J
♥ A K 10 9 5
♦ A K 10 6
♣ 10 7 3

South opened 1♥ and North bid 2♥. South optimistically tried for game bidding 3♦ and North bid 4♥. West led the ♠ 6.

Declarer won the ♠A and cashed the ♥AK. He started a crossruff; ♦AK, ruff a diamond, ruff a spade, ruff a diamond, and ruff a spade. But he lost the last four tricks, losing three clubs and a high trump.

Down one.

Unlucky or overbid?

A little of both but with proper technique, declarer has ten tricks. If he counts his tricks and entries, he will start his crossruff at Trick 2. After winning the opening lead, ruff a spade back to his hand. Now proceed exactly the same as the above declarer.

But that extra spade ruff is the tenth trick. On the last three tricks, the defenders high clubs and high trump clash together.

Making four hearts.

DEAL # 62   DO WHAT YOU MUST

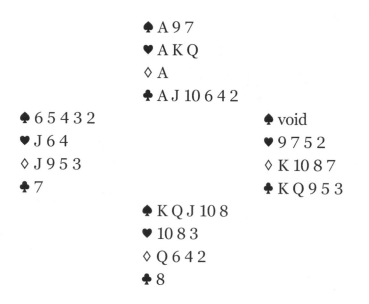

♠ A 9 7
♥ A K Q
◊ A
♣ A J 10 6 4 2

♠ 6 5 4 3 2
♥ J 6 4
◊ J 9 5 3
♣ 7

♠ void
♥ 9 7 5 2
◊ K 10 8 7
♣ K Q 9 5 3

♠ K Q J 10 8
♥ 10 8 3
◊ Q 6 4 2
♣ 8

North opened 1♣ and South bid 1♠. North bid 2♥. When South rebid 2♠, North drove to 6♠ after asking for Keycards and the trump queen. West led a trump.

Declarer won the trump lead and started to plan. With ten top tricks, he needed two ruffs in dummy. But this would require a crossruff since his hand lacked entries. He cashed the ◊A, then the ♥AK. West played the ♥J on the second heart.

Declarer started the crossruff, reluctant to try to cash a third high heart. West discarded a heart on the second club and declarer was doomed.

Good false-card from West but would you have been fooled?

It doesn't matter. If you need to cash three high hearts, just do it. No better line of play presents itself so just give West a "you can't fool me" look and proceed with your plan.

Nice try, Mr. West but not today. Making six spades.

DEAL # 63   OVERCOMING GOOD DEFENSE

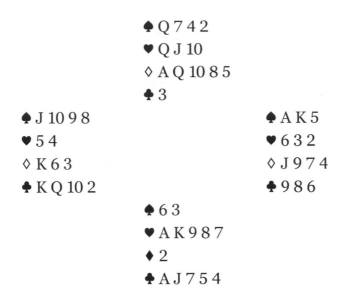

♠ Q 7 4 2
♥ Q J 10
◊ A Q 10 8 5
♣ 3

♠ J 10 9 8
♥ 5 4
◊ K 6 3
♣ K Q 10 2

♠ A K 5
♥ 6 3 2
◊ J 9 7 4
♣ 9 8 6

♠ 6 3
♥ A K 9 8 7
♦ 2
♣ A J 7 5 4

South opened 1♥ and reached 4♥ after a two-over-one auction. West led the ♥ 4.

Declarer won in dummy. What about setting up the diamonds? If they were 4-3, declarer could set them up but lacked an entry back. Maybe he could ruff out a short ◊K.

Good ideas, but unsuccessful. He finished with nine tricks.

Was there a better operation?

Without that good opening lead, you would have ten tricks with ease. So win the opening lead in hand, which seems contrary to your normal instincts, and take a diamond finesse.

If it wins, go back to Plan A and go about your crossruff for ten tricks.

DEAL # 64 DO WHAT YOU GOTTA DO

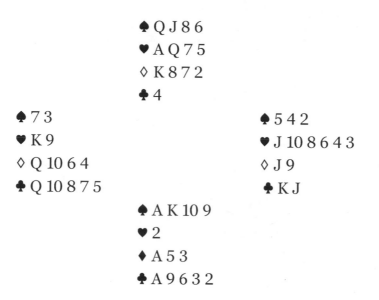

♠ Q J 8 6
♥ A Q 7 5
◊ K 8 7 2
♣ 4

♠ 7 3
♥ K 9
◊ Q 10 6 4
♣ Q 10 8 7 5

♠ 5 4 2
♥ J 10 8 6 4 3
◊ J 9
♣ K J

♠ A K 10 9
♥ 2
♦ A 5 3
♣ A 9 6 3 2

South opened 1♣ and North bid 1♦. South bid 1♠. North's 4♣ bid was a splinter raise of spades, showing club shortness. With his control rich hand and his own singleton, South checked for Keycards and reached 6♠. West led the ♠ 3.

Without a trump lead, South had an easy twelve tricks. He tried setting up his club suit but even if clubs divided, he used up all his entries.

Down one.

Do you see a road to twelve tricks?

Yes, an annoying lead. Take the simple road; a heart finesse at Trick 2. If it wins, go about your crossruff.

If it loses, don't call me. Go on to the next hand.

DEAL # 65   WHOOPS

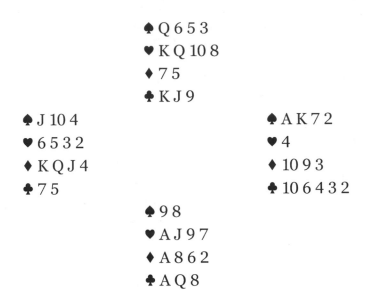

♠ Q 6 5 3
♥ K Q 10 8
♦ 7 5
♣ K J 9

♠ J 10 4
♥ 6 5 3 2
♦ K Q J 4
♣ 7 5

♠ A K 7 2
♥ 4
♦ 10 9 3
♣ 10 6 4 3 2

♠ 9 8
♥ A J 9 7
♦ A 8 6 2
♣ A Q 8

South opened 1NT and reached 4♥ after a Stayman auction. West led the ♦ K.

Declarer counted eight winners and saw this deal as a crossruff. If he could score two ruffs in each hand, one diamond, three clubs, and two high trumps, he had ten tricks. At Trick 2, he returned a diamond.

West won and returned a trump. Declarer won and ducked a spade. But when he tried to cash three high clubs, West ruffed. Down one.

Was this a crossruff? If not, what kind was it?

You start with eight top tricks and need two ruffs. If you ruff two spades in hand, like a dummy reversal, there is no need to risk cashing three clubs.

Lose two spades, cross to dummy and ruff two spades in hand. You can draw trumps with the remaining high trumps in dummy.

Note: If the defenders win a spade and cash one diamond followed by another diamond, declarer can ruff two diamonds in the dummy instead of two spades in the South hand for ten tricks.

DEAL # 66   WATCH THOSE ENTRIES

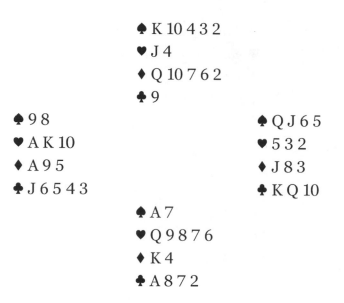

```
                        ♠ K 10 4 3 2
                        ♥ J 4
                        ♦ Q 10 7 6 2
                        ♣ 9
        ♠ 9 8                             ♠ Q J 6 5
        ♥ A K 10                          ♥ 5 3 2
        ♦ A 9 5                           ♦ J 8 3
        ♣ J 6 5 4 3                       ♣ K Q 10
                        ♠ A 7
                        ♥ Q 9 8 7 6
                        ♦ K 4
                        ♣ A 8 7 2
```

South opened 1♥ and North bid 1♠. When South rebid 2♣, North took a preference to 2♥, ending the auction. West led the ♠ 9.

Declarer made the natural play, winning the ace. He played the ♣A and ruffed a club. Then he tried to ruff another club. Both defenders quickly pointed out, "You are on the board."

With no sure way back to his hand, there was no second club ruff. Down one.

Did you keep the necessary entry?

If you won the opening lead on the board, seemingly contrary to usual, you preserved an entry to your hand for a second club ruff for your eighth trick.

Two spades, two hearts with those spots, one diamond, two club ruffs and the club ace is eight tricks. Of course, if West had been alert to the auction, he might have led the ♥AK.

Where would South's tricks come from now? Nowhere.

DEAL # 67   WHAT CAN GO WRONG?

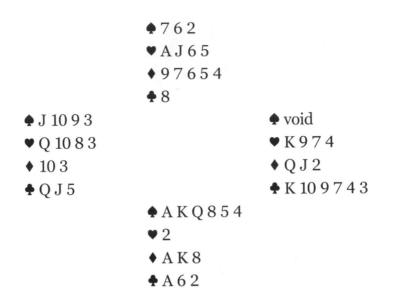

♠ 7 6 2
♥ A J 6 5
♦ 9 7 6 5 4
♣ 8

♠ J 10 9 3
♥ Q 10 8 3
♦ 10 3
♣ Q J 5

♠ void
♥ K 9 7 4
♦ Q J 2
♣ K 10 9 7 4 3

♠ A K Q 8 5 4
♥ 2
♦ A K 8
♣ A 6 2

South opened 2♣, strong and artificial. After North bid 2♦, waiting, South bid 2♠. When North bid 3♠ showing trump support and some outside values, South checked for Keycards and outside kings and stopped in 6♠. West led the ♥ 3.

Declarer won the opening lead and cashed the ♠A. The contract could no longer be made. Declarer cashed the ♣A and ruffed a club. He ruffed a heart, ruffed a club, and ruffed another heart. He had a diamond loser and a trump loser at the end. Down one.

Do you see how you could have insured the contract?

After winning the opening lead, ruff a heart at Trick 2. This seemingly innocuous play allows declarer to ruff three hearts in hand, scoring six trump tricks in hand and two club ruffs in dummy.

With the ♥A, the ♦AK, and the ♣A, that's twelve tricks total.

DEAL # 68   WHICH SUIT FIRST?

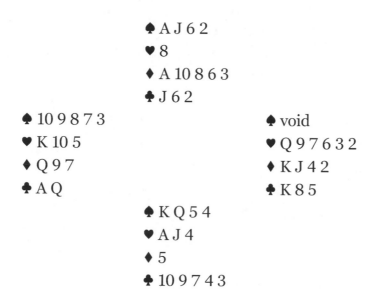

$\spadesuit$ A J 6 2
$\heartsuit$ 8
$\diamondsuit$ A 10 8 6 3
$\clubsuit$ J 6 2

$\spadesuit$ 10 9 8 7 3
$\heartsuit$ K 10 5
$\diamondsuit$ Q 9 7
$\clubsuit$ A Q

$\spadesuit$ void
$\heartsuit$ Q 9 7 6 3 2
$\diamondsuit$ K J 4 2
$\clubsuit$ K 8 5

$\spadesuit$ K Q 5 4
$\heartsuit$ A J 4
$\diamondsuit$ 5
$\clubsuit$ 10 9 7 4 3

After two passes, East opened 2$\heartsuit$ passed to North who reopened with a take-out double. South bid 2$\spadesuit$, then 3$\spadesuit$ when West competed with 3$\heartsuit$. West led the $\spadesuit$ 10.

Declarer won in hand, cashed the $\heartsuit$A and ruffed a heart. He cashed the $\diamondsuit$A and ruffed a diamond. Then a heart ruff and another diamond ruff. But now he was in his hand with nothing to ruff.

There was a high trump in each hand, but he could not score them separately. Declarer only had eight tricks. Down one.

What went wrong? How could this have been prevented?

When contemplating a crossruff, it is often crucial to decide which suit goes first. In this deal, if declarer starts the diamonds, he ends up in the dummy and can ruff one more diamond, separating the remaining two trump.

Nine tricks if you start properly.

DEAL # 69   WATCH THOSE ENTRIES

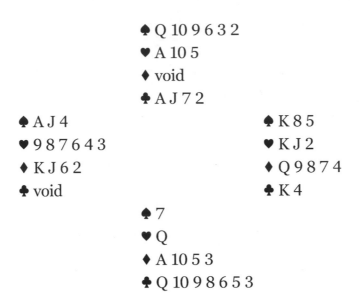

♠ Q 10 9 6 3 2
♥ A 10 5
♦ void
♣ A J 7 2

♠ A J 4
♥ 9 8 7 6 4 3
♦ K J 6 2
♣ void

♠ K 8 5
♥ K J 2
♦ Q 9 8 7 4
♣ K 4

♠ 7
♥ Q
♦ A 10 5 3
♣ Q 10 9 8 6 5 3

North opened 1♠ and South bid 1NT, forcing for one round. North rebid 2♠. South considered passing but bid 3♣. North bid 5♣. West led the ♥ 9.

Declarer won the opening lead and played the ♣A. Leaving the ♣K out, South began crossruffing, hearts in the South hand, diamonds in the North hand.

He reached the point where he needed to cross back to his hand to ruff his last diamond but had no entry. He led a spade. East won and cashed the ♣K.

No more ruffs, down one.

And the solution is?

At Trick 2, lead a spade. Whichever defender wins this trick cannot lead a trump. Then play continues as above except declarer can ruff one more diamond.

Eleven tricks!

DEAL # 70   OPENING LEAD PROBLEM

West
♠ K J 8
♥ A K
♦ K Q 10 6 2
♣ K 9 3

West	North	East	South
1♦	2♦	P	2♥
All Pass			

What is your opening lead?

If you led the ♦ King, -110. Declarer won the opening lead. She scored two spade ruffs in hand, three trump tricks in the dummy, and 3 outside aces; eight tricks. If declarer risks a spade finesse, -140. If you led a club or spade, same result.

What is the best lead against two-suited hands, especially when a possible crossruff is coming? Trumps! If you led two rounds of hearts, declarer is limited to six tricks. Well done.

North
♠ A Q 9 5 3
♥ Q J 9 8 3
♦ 9
♣ 8 6

South
♠ 4
♥ 10 7
♦ A 8 7 5 4
♣ A 7 5 4 2

DEAL # 71   WHO NEEDS THEM

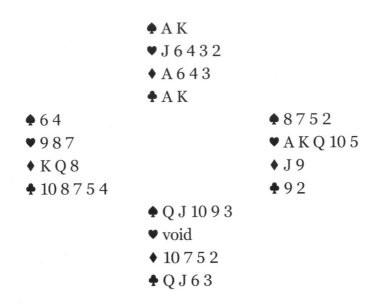

♠ A K
♥ J 6 4 3 2
♦ A 6 4 3
♣ A K

♠ 6 4
♥ 9 8 7
♦ K Q 8
♣ 10 8 7 5 4

♠ 8 7 5 2
♥ A K Q 10 5
♦ J 9
♣ 9 2

♠ Q J 10 9 3
♥ void
♦ 10 7 5 2
♣ Q J 6 3

After East opened 2♥, North-South reach 4♠. West led the ♥ 9.

South ruffed the opening lead and cashed the ♠AK. He then cashed the ♣AK and ruffed a heart. When he tried to draw the remaining trumps and West discarded, declarer was doomed.

Down two.

Was declarer unlucky or could he have survived in his 5-2 fit?

Declarer didn't think about what kind of hand this was, and he failed to count his tricks. After ruffing the opening lead, cash the ♣AK. Cash the ♦A and start crossruffing hearts, ruffing the good clubs as entries to the dummy.

Seven trump tricks plus the ♣AK and ♦A comes to ten tricks. No problem.

DEAL # 72   HANDLING THE 4-3 FIT

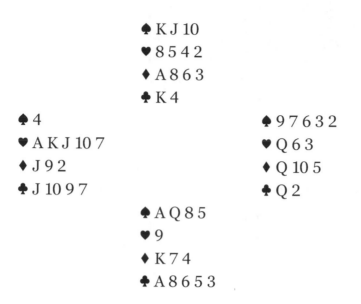

♠ K J 10
♥ 8 5 4 2
♦ A 8 6 3
♣ K 4

♠ 4
♥ A K J 10 7
♦ J 9 2
♣ J 10 9 7

♠ 9 7 6 3 2
♥ Q 6 3
♦ Q 10 5
♣ Q 2

♠ A Q 8 5
♥ 9
♦ K 7 4
♣ A 8 6 5 3

South opened 1♣ and West overcalled 1♥. North had a difficult bid, finally choosing a negative double. When South jumped to 3♠, North bid 4♠. West led the ♥ A.

At Trick 2, West switched to a trump. Declarer decided this was a second suit hand and tried to set up the clubs. He won Trick 2 in dummy and cashed the ♣AK. He ruffed a club and played a diamond to his ace. He ruffed another club with dummy's last trump.

But when he tried to draw trump, he lost control of the hand. The defense cashed the remaining hearts and two trump tricks. Painful.

How might you have handled this 4-3 fit?

Possession of all the high trump honors makes this hand not difficult at all. After the trump switch, cash the ♦AK, the ♣AK and crossruff all five of the remaining trumps.

You score six trump tricks and four top minor winners.

DEAL # 73   ANOTHER TOUCHY 4-3

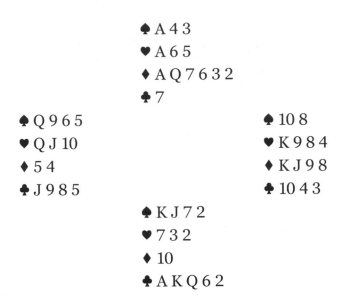

♠ A 4 3
♥ A 6 5
♦ A Q 7 6 3 2
♣ 7

♠ Q 9 6 5
♥ Q J 10
♦ 5 4
♣ J 9 8 5

♠ 10 8
♥ K 9 8 4
♦ K J 9 8
♣ 10 4 3

♠ K J 7 2
♥ 7 3 2
♦ 10
♣ A K Q 6 2

South opened 1♣ and rebid 1♠ after North bid 1♦. North bid 2♥, fourth suit game forcing. South bid 3♣ and North bid 3♠. South bid 4♠. West led the ♥ Q.

Declarer won the ace and tried drawing trump with a finesse to his jack. West won the queen and cashed two rounds of hearts. The ♠9 was the setting trick.

Could you have handled this 'touchy' trump fit?

When looking at short suits in both hands plus a 'touchy' trump suit, think about a crossruff. Count your sure tricks just like in notrump. You have seven: two spades, one heart, one diamond, and three clubs. Not so bad. You only need three ruffing tricks.

Try cashing three rounds of clubs (62%) and discard two hearts. Now ruff a heart (ruffing trick #1). Cash the ♦A and ruff a diamond (ruffing trick #2). Ruff another heart in dummy (ruffing trick #3). Since West didn't overcall 1♥, hearts are likely 4-3.
You have taken the first eight tricks and still have the ♠AKJ. Can you take two more tricks?

DEAL # 74   TAKE WHAT YOU CAN

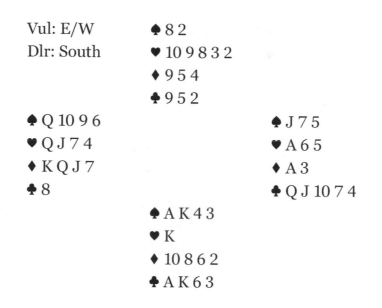

Vul: E/W
Dlr: South

	♠ 8 2	
	♥ 10 9 8 3 2	
	♦ 9 5 4	
	♣ 9 5 2	
♠ Q 10 9 6		♠ J 7 5
♥ Q J 7 4		♥ A 6 5
♦ K Q J 7		♦ A 3
♣ 8		♣ Q J 10 7 4
	♠ A K 4 3	
	♥ K	
	♦ 10 8 6 2	
	♣ A K 6 3	

South opened 1♣ rather than 1NT since he had four spades so no rebid problem. West doubled for take-out and East, with no suit to bid and good clubs passed for penalty. West led the ♣ 8.

Declarer won the opening lead and cashed the ♠AK. He ruffed a spade in dummy and led a heart. East won and returned a trump. Declarer finished with five tricks, minus 300, not a very good result.

Could you have done better?

You cannot make seven tricks, but down one, minus 100, would be a reasonable result. The opponents can certainly make a part-score. At Trick 2, lead the heart king. East will win and return a trump. But now declarer can ruff a heart back to his hand for a sixth trick.

Sometimes a secondary goal, when you cannot make your contract, is worth trying to achieve. East-West have a decent play for 2NT, even 3NT if they drop the singleton heart king.

DEAL # 75   AVOIDING THE TRUMP SHIFT

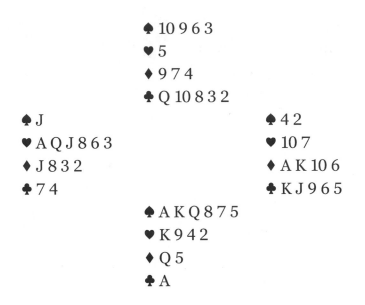

♠ 10 9 6 3
♥ 5
♦ 9 7 4
♣ Q 10 8 3 2

♠ J
♥ A Q J 8 6 3
♦ J 8 3 2
♣ 7 4

♠ 4 2
♥ 10 7
♦ A K 10 6
♣ K J 9 6 5

♠ A K Q 8 7 5
♥ K 9 4 2
♦ Q 5
♣ A

South opened 1♠ and West overcalled 3♥. After two passes, South bid 3♠ and North raised to 4♠. West led the ♦ 2.

East cashed the ♦AK and shifted to a trump, something perhaps he should have done at Trick 2. South won the ace. Needing to ruff hearts, he led a low heart. West ducked since he had no trump and East won.

He returned his last trump. Declarer could only ruff two hearts in dummy for nine tricks. Down one.

Can you find a way home if East makes the same slip at Trick 2?

When East returned a trump at Trick 3, what did West play? The jack. If that's an honest card, and why not, it's a singleton. When declarer leads a heart, lead the king! Who do you think has the ace? West wins, but the defense is helpless.

Notice if East returns a trump at Trick 2. When West gets in with a heart, he can lead to East's other high diamond honor. Now another trump lead by East and declarer can no longer ruff three hearts.

DEAL # 76   AN UNUSUAL FINESSE

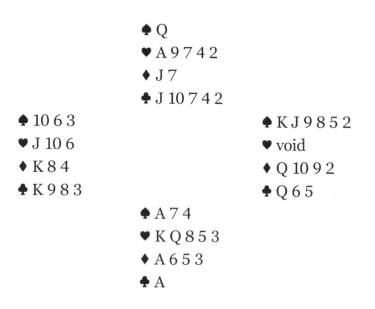

♠ Q
♥ A 9 7 4 2
♦ J 7
♣ J 10 7 4 2

♠ 10 6 3   ♠ K J 9 8 5 2
♥ J 10 6   ♥ void
♦ K 8 4   ♦ Q 10 9 2
♣ K 9 8 3   ♣ Q 6 5

♠ A 7 4
♥ K Q 8 5 3
♦ A 6 5 3
♣ A

South opened 1♥. When North bid 4♥, South bid 6♥. West led the ♥ 6.

Declarer correctly tried for a crossruff. But after two club ruffs and two spade ruffs, he had to play the ♦A and a diamond. West won and played another trump, leaving declarer a trick short.

Could you have survived this good defense?

You could take a finesse. What finesse you ask? A spade finesse. West made a good opening lead and you have to let the opponents regain the lead one more time. If in diamonds, another trump is coming back.

But if you lead a low spade and East has to win the trick, he has no trump to play. Later you can discard dummy's diamond loser on the spade ace.

Nine trump tricks and three aces, losing one unexpected spade.

Printed in the United States
by Baker & Taylor Publisher Services